IN THE PUBLIC INTEREST

The Life of Robert Emmet Lee From the FBI to the FCC

Robert Emmet Lee

with

John Shosky

University Press of America, Inc.
Lanham • New York • London

Copyright © 1996 by
University Press of America,® Inc.
4720 Boston Way
Lanham, Maryland 20706

3 Henrietta Street
London, WC2E 8LU England

ISBN 0-7618-0193-6 (cloth: alk: ppr.)

TABLE OF CONTENTS

COLLABORATOR'S NOTE

Robert E. Lee lived a singular life. He was a favorite of J. Edgar Hoover, and was present at the dawn of the Federal Bureau of Investigation. He was a close friend of Joseph McCarthy, and watched the tragedy of McCarthy's self-destruction. He then became one of the architects of modern telecommunications policy, while serving as a Presidential appointee at the Federal Communications Commission for more than 27 years. This is the longest record of appointed service at that particular regulatory agency, and perhaps the longest number of years in appointed service to our country by anyone in this century. In any of these capacities, Mr. Lee would have a terrific story to tell. Weaving them together, he spins quite a yarn.

At his death in 1993, Mr. Lee left a completed manuscript. However, it needed editing and polishing. Therefore, Mrs. Rose Bente Lee, his wife, hired me to put the manuscript into a publishable form. This book would not have been possible without Mrs. Lee's persistence, guidance, and generosity. Graciously, she has consented to list me as a collaborator. But, I must add, that this is Mr. Lee's book, start to finish.

Mr. Lee was advised in the preparation of this manuscript by the late Milton Lomask, who deserves much credit for his supervisory efforts. My own work has been greatly assisted by Heather Garnos, Paul Summers, Austin Shepherd, Robert Barnard, and Matt Peterson of Roncalli Communications. I have also benefitted greatly from conversations with Kathryn Jo Ottman and Elizabeth Stolpe. I should thank Ross and Betty Macmillan, Lucy Macmillan, and Jeff and Judy Fuller who provided a peaceful setting for preparation of this manuscript.

I must recognize the assistance of the George Mason University School of Law Library, the American University Computer

Center, the Library of Congress, Kathy Heinz, and Melissa Gentry. Dr. David Rodier, Kellene Kennedy, and the faculty of the Department of Philosophy and Religion at the American University have been most kind in their encouragement and support.

Several of Mr. Lee's friends have been extremely generous with their time and guidance. I thank each one of them, especially Vincent Curtis, Peggy Reed Greene, James Quello, Ward Quaal, Marvin Rosenberg, Stanley Hubbard, Tommy Scott, Lee Lovenger, Rose Marie Borda, Thomas Dougherty, and David Ryan.

Finally, I would like to thank Mrs. Rose Lee and the Lee family for their faith and trust. Bob's story deserves to be placed in print. I am honored to have been of service. As Mr. Lee dedicated his own work to his family, I remember David, Kellene, and my academic family at the American University.

PREFACE

I write this at the end of my life. This book is a reflection in the mirror, the pictures of memory. But as St. Patrick cast out the snakes, so I cast aside any hesitation to speak. This is my life and the lessons I've learned, from the streets of Chicago to the offices of the Federal Bureau of Investigation, in the halls of Congress and the chambers of the Federal Communications Commission. I've had a unique vantage point in the formation of our political system and our culture. This book attempts to capture the sands through the hourglass, and highlight some of the lessons we must learn from our history.

I dedicate this book to my family -- our love is eternal.

1

IRISH IN CHICAGO

We remember strange and wonderful things about our childhood. I vividly recall a plaque hanging in my mother's kitchen which read

> "There is so much good in the worst of us
> And so much bad in the best of us
> That it behooves none of us
> To speak about the rest of us."

That thought strictly governed my home. We were taught that each person is fallible; each one of us confronts the trials of life. So we must be tolerant, forgiving, and charitable -- that person in need could be anyone, including you or me.

Naturally, there is a great deal of tolerance in the Irish, and we were Irish in Chicago. We were the "Old Sod" planted in the New World. Both of my parents, Patrick Joseph Lee and the former Delia Ryan, grew up in small villages near Galway Bay. The song immortalizing that body of water was often sung in the Lee household. Father came from Garrynagry; Mother from Rosscahill. Both were baptized with the holy water in the same church; both went to school together in the parish of Kilhannin.

Mother's family appears to have been well-to-do, but as the last of thirteen children, she inherited nothing under British law. I believe that both of her parents died during infancy and her upbringing fell to older siblings. When such misfortunes occurred in her day girls were sent to a nunnery at the earliest possible age. Seven of my mother's sisters were dispatched to marriage with the church, some of them subsequently coming to the United States on the sailing ships that were once the lifeline between continents. Mother was put in a convent, but she did not stay put. One night she slipped out of the nunnery, somehow raised passage money, and came to America. But God watched over this slim girl in her late teens, giving her strength and determination. I believe it was no coincidence that in this country she met her childhood neighbor, married him, and became the proud parent of three girls -- Margaret, Mildred (Later Sister Cecilia, B.V.M.), and Elanore -- and two boys -- Edward and myself.

****

I have often wondered if my parents even knew of the celebrated, revered Civil War General who is often thought to be a distant relative. Many people persist in believing in some connection. Shortly after my confirmation in 1954 to the first of what were to be four terms on the Federal Communications Commission (FCC), a Senator from one of the southern states revealed he had voted for me "against my better judgment." Naturally, I wondered why. "Because," he said, "you're a nephew, grandson, or some such thing of General Lee."

"But that's all nonsense," I protested. "I'm Robert E. (for Emmet) Lee, a second-generation Irishman from the back streets of Chicago."

"I know that, my boy, " said the Senator, "but I'm not sure my constituents do, and they'd never forgive me for voting against Robert E. Lee."

Well, the truth is that I was named for a rebel -- but not from the American Civil War. A friend living in our largely Irish corner of Chicago took umbrage at my parents for naming my older brother Edward, after one of my mother's brothers. Our neighbor thought that Edward had an English sound, and he implored mother, should another boy appear, to give him a "truly Irish moniker." Sadly, our friend died before my arrival, and my mother felt obligated to honor his request. So she named me for the fiery nineteenth-century Dubliner, executed by the English in his twenty-fifth year for his part in an unsuccessful rebellion against colonial rule.

There was a streak of the rebel in us, as with most Irish. When my father arrived on American soil in 1893, he stepped on the docks at Boston, studiously glanced around him, and exclaimed: "If there's a government here, I'm agin it."

Those words often echoed in my mind during my tenure at the FCC. I strongly shared my father's Jeffersonian views. But the irony is that once Patrick Lee had settled in Chicago and received his citizenship papers, he proceeded to work for many years for the city government, first as a foot patrolman on the police force and later as a detective. I followed in my father's footsteps -- literally -- by becoming a special agent of the FBI, and then moving on to become a chief investigator for the Appropriations Committee of the House of Representatives, and finally accepting a Presidential Appointment to serve as a Commissioner of the FCC.

My arrival on March 31, 1912 placed me well into the second decade of this revolutionary century. But the values I heard at home came from an earlier era. My father believed that the best government is that which intrudes the least into our daily lives. He was a nineteenth century man, who believed the American Creed -- that in this country common men could do uncommon things. He had a bit of the frontier spirit in him, fueled by a

Patrick Joseph Lee.

Delia Ryan Lee.

belief that Uncle Sam should hold himself aloof from our lives, allowing each one of us to rise or fall through our own efforts, doing for us only those things we cannot do for ourselves. Dad would be pleased to see that our country is starting to come back to those values, closing the twentieth century by intellectually turning back to the nineteenth.

****

Brother Edward, he of the English name, was the first-born of the children, and by the time I showed up two of the three sisters were on hand. Though I began life in a small gas-lit flat above a tavern at Clark and Dewey Streets on Chicago's North Side, the home that dominates the memories of my childhood was the one we moved into when I was still a small boy -- a detached three-story frame house at 2327 Seminary Avenue in a section of North Chicago known as St. Vincent's Parish.

Of course, we weren't rich. But the great thing about this house was that it belonged to us. Dad was paying off the mortgage, and he managed to feed and clothe the lot of us on a policeman's salary of $50 a week. We didn't waste a penny, stretching that $50 as far as it could go. My brother Edward also helped later on, cutting short his education to take a job at American Express.

But we weren't poor, either. The word "poverty" was not part of our vocabulary and I do not remember wanting for a thing. While the neighborhood was under-privileged, there was no poverty as we know it today. People helped each other, because we all knew each other. We had an extended Irish family that included all the neighbors, all the Irish "micks." Many people today have never experienced the upside of "ethnicity," the strong sense of community, and the feeling of joint responsibility. As children we had our own parents and our adopted neighborhood parents. We took care of each other. We had to look out for one another. It was expected that no one be turned away. For instance, I was not aware of any relief available from the city. When catastrophe struck, the church and the neighbors assisted those in need, with some of us even taking in families from time to time. No one really expected government aid; we helped each other as needed. One sign of the times was a vagrancy law that permitted a person who had no visible means of support to be incarcerated. Of course, as America grew, and our ethnic neighborhoods dispersed, with each of us being integrated into the "melting pot" of American society, this sort of treatment of the poor became unmanageable. Now, many individuals do not have to share the sorrows of misfortune, and the community has less incentive to act in unison. Our country has lost a vital source of shared responsibility, and the resulting alienation of the individual is the cause of many social ills that have mushroomed in our time, with great expense to the taxpayers and far too little payback for the expenditures devoted to social programs. If we cannot count on our neighbors or our church -- the people who know us best -- then the government is a poor, if necessary, substitute.

Some people may think I look back through the past with a green tint on my spectacles, but it would be hard to over-exaggerate our Irishness. Our Seminary Avenue house stood in an almost wholly Catholic area, so overwhelmingly Irish that I reached the age of ten before I even realized that I was not brought up on the "Old Sod" itself. The neighborhood consisted of mostly municipal employees, along with a few blacksmiths and workers in the Chicago stockyards. There were some small merchants, but not many. Most of the adult Irish males sought and clung to salaried positions, fearful that if they went into business for themselves they might be unable to provide for their families. Most of the adults had known poverty in Ireland, and remained economically conservative.

There was great rapport among the occupants of the neighborhood -- the closeness common to newcomers to a strange land. We were people driven by a need to be with people of a similar background.   Chicago was like many other urban cities -- the immigrant Irish lived in an Irish section of town, the Italians lived in another area, the Slavs stayed close together, and so on.   We see that same pattern of ethnic proximity among the Asian and Hispanic immigrants that constitute the "new wave" drawn by the promise of the Statute of Liberty.   This is a land of opportunity, and often it is the strength of our surrounding community that turns a hopeful dream into a promising start in this mobile society.

In my neighborhood the best example of our ethnic heritage was the two- or three-day ordeal known as the "wake."   Because we all knew each other, our common grief demanded public relief. Illness or misfortune were quickly known through the grapevine, and word rapidly spread when a family called for a crepe on the door, the color speaking volumes about who had died, as the color indicated the approximate age of the deceased.   Afterwards, when the family was ready, an open coffin stood in the parlor or in the funeral home.   The neighbors would drop by to comfort the family with consoling words and to share the generous drafts of liquor that flowed on such an occasion.   Singing and public speeches were proper and expected.   A life departed became an almost ritualistic way of renewing the ties among the living.   Of course, things sometimes did get out of hand -- the consumption of ardent spirits leading to high jinx.   Many people came -- some of them previously unknown.   I know that some of the older lads used to comb the newspapers for the addresses of wakes and then go over for a free drink.   Unfortunately, the custom is fast disappearing, a victim of our disintegrating sense of community. Half saturnalia, half lamentation, the wake vouchsafed to the family of the deceased an opportunity to get rid of tensions and to bring grief under control.   It allowed for relatives and neighbors to fondly remember the life of a good man or woman, saying goodbye with thanksgiving for a life well-spent -- a life that touched everyone in the neighborhood.   I hope that my passing affords an excuse for a wake, because I know that my friends and family will have one for the history books.

[Collaborator's Note: on Mr. Lee's passing, a wake of epic proportions did take place. And, yes, they did sing "Galway Bay."]

****

If my parents had any serious faults, I've forgotten them. My father was a big man, a guy right out of John Ford's "The Quiet Man" -- with "shoulders like an ox." He was big in size and big in spirit. He had a big sense of humor and a big laugh. His biggest priority was his family and his faith. He was proud of us, and he wanted us to be proud of him. Once a month he had to undergo "inspection day" -- the day when uniformed officers were examined for their tidiness. The whole family got involved. The children polished the detachable buttons. Mother made certain the uniform was wrinkle-free and spotless. Dad polished his shoes and badge. Shiny and newly-brushed, off he'd go, pausing briefly at the door, as he did every morning, to lift his hat and make the sign of the cross. It was a family accomplishment that in all his years as a foot patrolman he was never disciplined for untidiness.

Dad was a good parent. He was always a great guy to have around, and I wasn't the only person to think so. So did my friends. At 2327 Seminary Avenue the basement was the entertainment room, the party place, and as I came into my upper teens my parents encouraged me to use it. The reasoning was sound -- it was better for me to raise hell under my own roof than out in the streets. So I would assemble a dozen of the lads. We'd put out a phone call or two, and soon have as many girls on hand. Then we'd whoop it up far into the night. On these occasions, my mother would retire to her bedroom, which was her way of saying that we were free to do as we wished. As for Pop -- sometimes he'd join her, but sometimes we'd ask him to join us. Everybody enjoyed his company. This is a far cry from today, when teenagers can't wait to get rid of the "old folks." We have lost the ability to have intergenerational fun. And when kids constantly leave home for their entertainment, we often lose our contact with their lives.

Mother was a remarkable parent, in her own way. My heart warms at the memory of her. She was always there, cooking and cleaning and entertaining the children with her stories of the Little People and other manifestations of the Irish imagination. She often said, proudly, that she had never spent so much as a day away from her own home. After all, in her eyes, being a mother was a full-time job, her half of the marriage pact. Keeping house was tough and time consuming. There was an old wood cooking stove in the kitchen and Mother heated irons over the open flames to press the clothes she'd washed on a scrub board. For many years the ancient heating stove had to be brought in and assembled every winter and taken away every spring. While the coming of steam was a monumental event to us, we continued to bank the fire in the furnace every night and stoke it up every morning. Mother often performed this task, too. In our day of modern conveniences, we soon forget the backbreaking work women performed in earlier times. Women like my mother sacrificed and gave and loved until there was nothing left to give - - my brothers and sisters are the product of her constant caring.

When Mother died, Dad sold the house at Seminary Avenue. The memories of her laughter and joy were more than his big heart could stand.

2

THE COMING OF RADIO

One day Edward strung a crude set of wires on our rooftop. He then attached this electronic mess to a home-made receiver, made of a hunk of crystal, a cat's whisker, wires, and an oatmeal box to wind it on. When this magical device caught a bit of music from one of the pioneer broadcasting stations, Edward and I called Mother into the room. Hearing sound coming from no visible source, she scolded us for making a fool of her. We hastily explained, and like millions of Americans, she became a devoted listener to radio.

It's hard to imagine the days of silence before radio. The noise from the streets and the sound of the family moving through the house were the noises of life. Then came radio, and the world came into our kitchen. Jack Benny, the Chicago White Sox, and Father Charles Coughlin seemed like old friends, waiting for us to turn on the radio. In fact, listening to the radio became one of Mother's great joys, bringing to her home a larger community of concerns and conversation. During my time as Commissioner, I remembered my mother's love of radio, and her willingness to make it part of her life. I remembered her faith, her trust, and the impact it had on her -- on all of us. That is why I wanted to constantly remind broadcaster's that they work for people like my mother -- the people who experience entertainment, information, and drama based on the decisions made by broadcasters. The impact of those decisions is so strong, so pervasive, and so lasting. Immense responsibility accompanies those decisions -- responsibility that is often ignored or forgotten.

***

Save for the radio, the world I grew up in was free of the mechanical distractions that have become the necessities of life today. We had no car, and never missed it. None of us had ever heard of a television set. We provided our own homemade and often very ingenious entertainment and a rich family life. We read just about everything we could put our hands on. And there was always the Church with its "socials", dances and organized sports.

I spent a considerable amount of time at home, listening to that radio, because at an early age I came down with some sort of chronic and rather serious illness. I describe it in these fuzzy terms because that was about all my good old doctor could make of it. Today, a modern doctor would find a cure quickly, since my troubles were very likely the result of a string of allergies like those suffered by my father and by one of my sons in his. For a few years I was racked by an almost constant cough and had to be carried around on a pillow. The only medicine that helped was a mixture of garlic and gin. Perhaps it was this introduction to a potent nectar at an early age that accounts for my subsequent ability to hold my liquor better than most.

During this period I wore clothing several times smaller than my age called for. This situation seemed to embarrass Mother. At any rate she fabricated a story to the effect that, according to the doctor, the coughing was giving me unusually strong lungs. Consequently, she asserted, I would grow up to be a giant of a fellow. That prediction, alas, failed to materialize. The about five foot ten to which I attained is considered diminutive in my family.

So it was not until my eighth year that I was well enough to enter school. This put me a grade or two behind my contemporaries, and in my annoyance I studied hard and got top-notch grades. I guess you have to reach a certain age before you realize how often what seem to be life's misfortunes are instead blessings in disguise.

I started my education at St. Vincent's Grammar School, taught by the Sisters of Charity, B.V.M., the order one of my sisters would enter later. I was a diligent student, but not a properly behaved one. Indeed in those days there seems to have been a capricious, mischievous "Till Eulenspiegel" in me. Like that much written about fourteenth century German rascal, I was given to what I considered merry pranks.

As I was leaving the building after school one day, for example, I noticed a nun correcting papers in an otherwise empty classroom. The door was closed, the key in the lock outside. Till Eulenspiegel took over and I turned the key and took off. Next day I learned that Sister was imprisoned for hours and terribly frightened. The authorities investigated but the culprit was never identified, and I can only hope that by now the statute of limitations has run out on this offense.

Other pranks followed, and when I was linked to some of them, a stocky German priest connected with the parish paid a call on my father. I wasn't present at this interview, but I gather that rough words flew, most of them emanating from Patrick Lee himself. In the end, Father showed his visitor the door and promptly arranged to remove me from St. Vincent's and enroll me at Knickerbocker, the public school of the neighborhood.

For me, this move had its costs and benefits. Some of the boys -- always, it seemed to me, the biggest ones -- saw fit to make slanderous remarks about Catholics, leaving me no choice but to put up my "dukes." I was pretty fair at fisticuffs, but I lacked heft.

My memory is that most of these battles went to the enemy. As word spread, however, that I stood ready to fight, the tauntings ebbed. Otherwise things went well. I was elected mayor of the student government and chief of the police force, whose duty it was to cover the corners near school and protect the other children as they came and went. It was pleasant sitting in classes containing girls as well as boys.

Best of all, since academically the public school lagged behind my old parochial institution, I was almost immediately advanced one grade, a change that put me on a level with my counterparts. Alas, this benign situation was not to last. During my second year at Knickerbocker a couple of nuns from St. Vincent's called on my father. Using tactics somewhat smoother than those of the stocky German priest, they persuaded him that the time had come to rescue his son from those "Protestants." Once back at St. Vincent's, I was promptly demoted to my former grade.

***

My brush with anti-Catholicism at Knickerbocker was not my only encounter with bigotry at an early age. I happen to be "Black Irish," a term applied to those of us who, instead of having light-colored eyes and hair, have dark eyes and hair. Many tales have been spun in an effort to account for our origins. One story traces them to England's defeat of the Spanish Armada in 1588 when numbers of Spanish sailors escaped into Ireland and merged with the natives. Another has it that in ancient times the fishing village of Galway, near where my parents grew up, was to a large extent populated by Frenchmen.

So pronounced are my own black-Irish features that I have at times been mistaken for someone who is Jewish. I remember in my younger years being razzed about this by schoolmates. I also remember an incident involving my father and one of the men who delivered ice in our neighborhood. It occurred on a St.

Patrick's Day when every true Hibernian sports a bit of green on his person. The ice man, ambling by with his horse and wagon, saw me playing outside our house and, spotting my bit of green, bellowed at me: "Take off that shamrock, you little sheeny." Alarmed and baffled, I ran into the house crying. Pop was working nights at the time and was in bed asleep. I woke him up and tearfully told him what had happened. I can see him yet, pulling on his trousers and dashing from the house, his suspenders billowing after him. Rapidly catching up with the ice man, he trounced him thoroughly, while I watched in glee from a distance.

Young and vulnerable as I was then, incidents of this sort upset me. Today I see them in a different light. My experiences as a target of discrimination have left me deeply averse to judging any person on the basis of his or her race, color, or religion. I know how much that sort of thing hurts. As for the ice man's barbaric yawp at me, I can only wonder if that occurrence meant what I now think it did. I didn't know the man, but I assume he lived either in our neighborhood or in one of the other immigrant-created enclaves common to the northern and western reaches of Chicago in the early twentieth century. These bailiwicks were like small towns. You could live your life in one of them and hardly ever see anyone different from yourself. Not until I reached high school did I meet someone Jewish of my own age. I now know that anti-Semitism needs no object, that it has a life of its own, that if all the Jews in the world were to vanish tomorrow, anti-Semitism would go virulently on.

I had met older Jewish Americans, though, and I had good reasons for liking them. When I was about twelve, my brother Ed was hired as auditor of the Lake Shore Gold and Country Club on the North Shore and arranged it so that I could caddie there when I had the time. The members were good tippers. Some of their names appeared often on the front pages of Chicago's newspapers. I remember the Loeb and Leopold families and how my heart bled for them as they endured the terrible tragedy of the Bobby Franks murder.   Another member was Albert D. Lasker, one of the owners of the Chicago Cubs.   He and his wife, Mary, later became leading sponsors of medical research.

One member I especially liked was Julius Rosenwald, a very rich man who spent millions providing better schools for blacks and promoting racial understanding.   He seemed to like me too. Although very old and only playing a few holes at a time, he came to the club often.   He retained me as his private caddie and paid me $20 a week just to be on call.   He once asked me to deliver a set of golf clubs he was giving to Chicago's police chief -- an Irishman of course.   It took me much of the day to make the trip to the North Shore and back downtown but at least I expected a big tip.   Surprise! I was ushered into the chief's august presence, patted on the head, and complimented for being the son of one of Chicago's Finest.   But no tip.   A cheap Irishman if I ever saw one.

Eddie Loos, the club's pro, once asked me to caddie for him in a Professional Golfers Association tournament at Evanston.   It was a two-day 36-hole event.   Coming through the rain to the last hole Eddie needed a birdie to tie the leader, McDonald Smith.   He promised me $100 if he succeeded.   His approach shot was beautiful, stopping only a few feet from the hole.   But the tournament ground rules wouldn't allow him to clean some mud off the ball and his putt rimmed the cup, breaking my heart and cutting my fee in half.

***

By the time I had reached the eighth grade, I had made up my mind to get my secondary education at the high school division of De Paul University.   As this was a private institution and would require more money than Pop could manage, I talked myself into a job at Brown's, a neighborhood drug store at 1100 Fullerton Avenue.   Every other day I reported for duty after school and worked until 11:00 P.M. Every other Saturday I was on duty from 9:00 A.M. until 11:00 P.M. For these exertions I received nine dollars one week and eleven the next. At my age and in those times, this was good pay. The job was beneficial in other ways. It kept me off the streets and there were sufficient lulls in the business to let me crack the books and keep up with schoolwork.

What I most fondly remember about Brown's was its club-like atmosphere. It was not just a place where prescriptions were filled. It was a neighborhood gathering place, what we today call an "old-fashioned" drug store, a kind that no longer exists. People came in to discuss their problems, medical and otherwise. We did a great deal of what is called "counter prescribing." This practice, I learned later, was frowned upon by the doctors of the area, but most of our customers could not afford a doctor for their minor ills.

I've grown to greatly appreciate physicians, but during those years at the drug store I saw some practices that put me to wondering. A surprisingly high number of prescriptions the physicians asked us to fill were for "acetylsalicylic acid," which is simple aspirin. Available in liquid form, this was to be taken at the rate of a teaspoonful every three hours, after which a patient was to come back for a refill, each time paying us about a dollar for something he could have bought off the open shelves for ten cents.

I asked one of the neighborhood doctors about this and his rationalization was unconvincing, though one might be tempted to take it with a spoonful of acetylsalicylic acid. Most of his patients, he told me, were either suffering from nothing at all or were too ill to be helped. All of them, however, wanted some attention from him. So he prescribed a little aspirin, reasoning that though it might do no good, it could do no harm either.

Rubbing alcohol was a favorite with daily tipplers until the laws were amended so as to require the inclusion of an ingredient which though nonpoisonous made the drinker deathly ill.

As a duly accredited drug store, Brown's was entitled each month to some ten gallons of ethyl alcohol (200 proof) to be sold for medicinal purposes. Sold it was, but rarely for these purposes. Most of it was converted into anything a customer wanted -- gin, rum, bourbon, Scotch whiskey. These concoctions were effected by means of flavors. We would prepare a pint of gin, for example, by putting six ounces of alcohol in a pint bottle, adding a certain amount of juniper juice, filling the rest of the container with distilled water, and adding a squirt of glycerin for smoothness.

As each bottle of whatever we made sold for $1.50, the drug store stood to take in $450 a month provided it disposed of its entire stock of alcohol -- which it always did. As it cost us only $20 to make up our liquid potion, the profits were high. Still, we could have made even more money had we resorted to bootleg alcohol, but to the best of my knowledge we never did. I suppose the kindest thing that can be said of our "legal" bootlegging was that if we didn't sell the stuff, the customer would go to some dirty basement for "rotgut." Our product was pure, if not always palatable, and we could tell ourselves that we were serving the public well.

Profitable to both the drug store and the doctors of the neighborhood was another of the legitimate rackets spawned by Prohibition. Every month the drug store was permitted to buy ten cases of bourbon in pint bottles. These had to be accounted for with prescriptions from the doctors. Never, in my years at Brown's, did I see a patient with such a prescription. The doctors simply dropped by from time to time to fill out phony prescriptions, sometimes using names out of the phone book or my name or the names of some of my relatives. It would have been easy to expose this practice, but the government ignored it -

- a circumstance that led me to see it as part of a giant conspiracy to flout a law that should never have been put on the books. The drug store paid the government $1.25 a pint, and although ours was a low-income area, the customers were happy to give us $6 for each one. On a monthly basis the ten cases of bourbon retailed at $1,440. Of this the doctors got 50 percent or $720 and the government $300, and my boss, A.E. Brown, pocketed a profit of $420.

The same thing can be said of these shenanigans as has been said of our sale of accepted forms of alcohol and dope. We could have behaved worse. My boss, given the kind of front his store provided, could have made tons of money had he elected to do business with the city's bootleggers. He knew better than that, not wanting to attract the attention of one of Chicago's mobs.

* * *

It was during my second year at Brown's Drug Store that I met Wilma Rector, the girl who was to become my first wife. Except at the very beginning, I never addressed her as Wilma. She was quick to tell me that she disliked the name and I, in love and eager to oblige, re-christened her "Rex," the name by which almost everyone would know her for the rest of her life.

Born in Kirklin, a small town near Indianapolis, Rex had come to Chicago to study nursing at Columbus Hospital. Marriage was on my mind almost from the start. I believe it was on hers too. But we were very young -- she was fifteen, I was a year older. More to the point, silver and gold had we none. Consequently, the wedding day would not come along until eight years later. By then Rex, a Methodist by rearing, had converted to my religion.

But, in the Great Depression, how was a fellow to entertain his sweetheart on next to no money? Well, love finds a way. We strolled in Lincoln Park -- all too briefly, for except on Saturday nights, Rex had to be back in the hospital by nine o'clock. Sundays we usually managed a movie, financed by my corralling empty soft-drink bottles from around the house during the week and cashing them in. Sometimes Mother gave me a dollar for doing some scrubbing for her. That added soft drinks and a bite to eat to our weeknight strolls.

***

In the summer following my completion of high school in 1931, I quit my job and went "hoboing" with my friend Frank Bruscato. During the depression years this was the fashionable thing for young men just out of high school or college to do. Jobs were scarce wherever you were, and there was always the possibility that if you went far enough away, things might be a little better there. In my case, I think there was a pent-up urge to see the world.

Well, the world I saw alongside the gleaming rails and in the hobo "jungles" at the outskirts of towns was not a pleasant one. It was a world of illness, disease, and malnutrition. The glamour of the rails quickly wore off. Mostly, Frank and I rode the small platform between cars known as the blind. We tied handkerchiefs around our heads to keep the cinders out of our eyes and hair. So long as the train was moving we hung on for dear life. When it came almost to a stop we jumped off and ran like hell to avoid arrest, only to dash back and hop on again when it resumed motion. A small slip and you were dead or minus a portion of your anatomy.

Fortunately for me, my companion had some experience at this life. More to the point, he was big and strong and handy with his fists. He rescued me from several entanglements. Indeed, without Frank, I doubt if I would have survived the ordeal.

Did I learn anything? A little, I guess -- mostly about the so-called code of the jungles. If you look for a positive lesson, it is that sharing is important to survival. In the world of the hoboes, the jungle is an outdoor kitchen where utensils can be found hanging on the trees. No one steals them and when you finish using the place, you clean up. When you reach a jungle near mealtime, you contribute to the repast. As a rule your gift consists of meat or vegetables bummed from stores or homes or, in the case of hospitals, earned by mowing their lawns. Whatever you bring goes into the pot. The result is that famous alfresco specialty known as "mulligan stew."

Our original destination was California, where both of us figured we could make our fortunes. By the time we hit Colorado Springs, Colorado, however, we decided that a couple of weeks on the road was enough and turned back. The closer we got to home, the more eager we were to be there. At St. Louis, Missouri, we lucked onto a truck driver whose helper had walked out on him. He was carrying twenty tons of copper wire to Chicago and we arranged to help him unload in exchange for transportation. Because the wire was heavy, the remaining trip took time.

It seemed endless. After unloading the truck in Chicago, reached at noon on a steaming hot day, we had just enough strength to drag ourselves to the streetcar that carried us to our homes. Once in mine I stayed in bed for twenty-four hours while Mother babied me.

***

On my feet again, I went looking for work. This was not easily found in the Chicago of the 26 depression years, but by fall I had stumbled into enough odd jobs to let me begin night courses in business law and accounting at De Paul University.

hiers. We witnessed the comings and goings of people and
ir money. We didn't have to search for life's lessons -- they
re played out before us each day.

a fellow brought up in the relatively staid environs of an Irish
holic enclave on the North Side, the world of the hotel was a
v one -- new and enlightening. "They tell me you are wicked,"
rl Sandburg writes of Chicago in his famous poem of that
ne, "and I believe them, for I have seen your painted women
ler the gas lamps luring the farm boys." What I saw were
cles in the daily newspaper repeatedly quoting local politicians
vowing to cleanse the city of its sin and corruption. Come
httime and I saw some of those same politicos, painted women
their arms, registering at the Congress.

***

first year at the hotel, 1932, was the one in which the
mocratic Convention at Chicago nominated Franklin D.
osevelt for what was to be the first of his four terms in the
ite House. I remember Mr. Roosevelt being denied admittance
our Joseph Urban Room because he showed up without his
edo.

least FDR knew where to come. With its Peacock Alley, its
htclub (the Urban Room), its Merry-Go-Round and four other
s, the Congress of my day was a lively place. Famous dance
ds came and went -- bands headed by still-remembered artists
h as Vincent Lopez, Eddy Duchin, and Guy Lombardo. When
stand-up comic Ben Bernie appeared at the College Inn, he
Lopez staged a running exchange of phony insults. Bernie
uld accuse Lopez of faking the left hand at the piano.
ereupon Lopez, seating himself with a flourish, would rattle off
whole of the popular song "Lola" with his left hand.

933, Chicago began emerging from the depression largely due

3

HOTELS AND OTHER WORL

The student years are often full of drinking, m
a rite of passage. But for me it was a time for
changes in direction. I was also very consci(
make money, both to pay for my education anc
future. And for a year or so odd jobs kept me
University. Then my brother found me a ste;
Congress, one of the large hotels fronting on M
downtown Chicago. For a night student, the
perfect one, as I did not have to report on duty
P.M.

One important part of my education did not
classroom. At the Congress I began to learn th
the world of figures, columns, and bank deposi
I began to see that the use of money revealed
needs, behavior, and expectations of human b
trail was like a fascinating book of courage and
knew how to read it.

So, at 11:00 P.M., I became one of the
assembled at the front desk of the hotel. We
and, as members of what was known as th
System, we from time to time functioned a

to its sponsorship of a World's Fair which drew such crowds that its managers kept it going for two years. One of the stars of this extravaganza was Sally Rand, who elevated the striptease to an art form by doing it with fans. She lived at the Congress and I remember her frequent complaints connected with coming in late at night. Her gripe was that she had to use the Michigan Avenue entrance and walk the length of Peacock Alley still made up and in her costume -- a curious expression of modesty, I thought, following a day during which she regularly took off much of the costume, both at the Fair and at the Chicago Theater.

Another of the hotel's customers was the then highly popular comedienne and dancer Texas Guinan, who with her chorus of beautiful young girls was packing them in somewhere on the Near North Side. She and my brother, who headed our little group of auditors became close friends. To this day, Edward treasures an autographed photo from her, inscribed "Your business and mine are very much alike -- we both deal in figures."

The Fair drew conventions and the wildest of these was the American Legion. Its members turned over streetcars and molested women. I remember the hotel managers putting valuables in storage while that convention was in town. I also remember being chased down Peacock Alley by a legionnaire on a big white horse.

***

Hotels in those days enjoyed only a modest business. If the Congress were half full we were doing well, and if the cashier saw fit, people who checked in after midnight could be given a discount rate known as a "use rate." As I learned later one of the cashiers -- we'll call him Bill -- was making the most of this privilege. He charged the guest full rate, entered the use rate on the books, and pocketed the difference. It so happened that for a time I was assigned to Bill's job. When Bill learned that whenever I charged the full rate I entered the correct amount on the books, he took alarm. For one thing he saw his little racket about to disappear. For another, he feared detection since someone in the front office might notice how much more money I was turning in. One night, in an attempt to get me out of the picture, Bill lifted fifty dollars from my drawer while I was out for a snack. One of the bellboys saw him in the act and told me about it later. Meanwhile my brother, realizing that I was in the middle of an embarrassing situation, had taken me out of the cashier's cage. Bill then returned to it but apparently not for long. My understanding is that soon thereafter the full story came out and Bill, sacked from the Congress, was having trouble finding another job in the hotel field.

***

Soon after the repeal of Prohibition in 1933 I was transferred to a new duty called "liquor control" -- an operation developed by the Horwath brothers. Coming to the United States from Hungary, the Horwaths -- seven of them, I believe -- found work in hotel kitchens where they were struck by the waste connected with the preparation of food and at the amounts of it that were being pilfered. Subsequently, they organized an accounting firm called Horwath and Horwath, of which my brother was to become a senior partner. They specialized in the development of elaborate cost controls for food and liquor, and it was to their system for managing the expenses involved in the purveyance of liquor that I was assigned. One of my tasks was to devise ways of cutting down on waste. I remember spending considerable time figuring out whether it was cheaper to use a large or a small olive in a martini, taking into account the cost of gin and of the two sizes of olives. We settled for the small one.

The Horwath brothers' accounting firm, which grew into the seventh largest in the world, began to go downhill after merging with another firm in the late 1980s. One of the casualties was its pension fund. When that went down the drain, about 350 current employees and others who had already retired lost their pensions. Edward was one of those. Fortunately, he had other means of support, but it was tough on those who do not.

As persons who might never help themselves to money seem to think nothing of stealing whiskey, my main liquor-control job was to keep the bartenders reasonably honest. The effort involved, among other things, the deft use of a ruler to measure the contents of partly-filled bottles. Every day I prepared a report, showing what each of the hotel's five bars should have taken in vis-a-vis its actual receipts. By rotating the bartenders we acquired patterns of shortages. When these appeared we called in employees of the Pinkerton National Detective Agency to investigate. As a rule the Pinkertons functioned by having a man and a woman drink at the bar. If they caught a bartender with, shall we say, his hand in the bottle, he was fired.

By watering the whiskey the bartender could sometimes beat the system, and in an effort to discourage this dodge I devised a bit of hocus-pocus. I obtained an instrument for measuring the specific gravity of liquids and known as a hydrometer. Having no scientific background, I had no idea how to use this gadget. Nor could I read it. Still, when I dunked it in a bottle in the presence of a bartender, lifted it and examined it solemnly and muttered "Ah!" like a doctor confronting an interesting symptom, the bartender usually got the message. Thereafter, if he watered, he did so lightly. If he overdid it -- a practice easily detectable by tasting the stuff -- he got fired. No prosecution followed, for proving guilt was impossible. But the word got around and that bartender had trouble finding another job in his field.

During the Prohibition years the Congress Hotel's wine cellar, a famous one valued at $50,000, was boarded up by the authorities, who on occasion came around to see that it remained that way. With the coming of repeal, the hotel set out to get itself a splash in the press by inviting reporters to watch the boss break down the barred door with an axe. I was present to inventory the contents of the cellar and bring the books up to date. We anticipated having on hand a plentiful supply of rare old wines, but all we found were empty shelves lavishly festooned with cobwebs. Someone had made off with the stock. Who? I've often wondered at the failure of the hotel to demand an investigation or of the police to undertake one to find out.

***

By early 1934 I was working as assistant auditor at another Chicago hotel, the Great Northern. This was a much smaller house but for me the job was a step up, and in 1935, thanks to a tip from brother Edward, I obtained an even better job as resident auditor at the Roosevelt Hotel in St. Louis, Missouri. There my actual boss was the owner of the hotel, one of the several management outfits then known collectively as the American Bondholders Protective Committee, established by the United States Congress to help revitalize hotels and other properties crippled by the depression.

The salary was $175 a month plus room, board, and all the booze one could consume. This was a magnificent setup for a young bachelor. To make things even sweeter, the manager of the hotel, Jim Riner, and his wife, Ada, showed a great liking for me. With Ricky Seifert, the room clerk, I found a companionable roommate and a good friend. Still, I was not happy. I hated St. Louis's suffocating summers, so hot that, according to the local wiseacres, were a dog to chase a rabbit across town they would proceed at a walk. I was at once homesick and love-sick. I missed brassy, bombastic Chicago. And I missed Rex, the girl I had left behind there.

When, in 1936, the American Bondholders Protective Committee offered me a job at its headquarters in the raunchy old City by the

Lake, I grabbed it. At the same time I arranged for Rex to join me in St. Louis. There, on a hot July day, my last day in that town, we were married at an early Mass at the St. Louis Cathedral.

As neither of our parents had as yet been informed, we had decided to keep the marriage a secret for the time being. Somehow that didn't pan out. On the day before, my last at the hotel, the word got around. The bellboys subjected me to all the hazing proper to such events. They and the other employees took up a collection and delegated the chief engineer to buy us a gift. It was a handsome coffee service. Only later did I learn that the engineer kept the money and charged the gift to the hotel. I suppose you would say that our first wedding present was "hot."

On the day of the wedding, Rex and I rose at 5:00 A.M. and walked from the hotel to the Cathedral. I don't remember the name of the priest, only that he was a paragon of beaming geniality. On learning that I had forgotten the need for a witness, he persuaded an elderly lady, the only other person in the church at the time, to perform that service. At the close of the Mass, I handed him an envelope containing twenty dollars. The new Mrs. Robert E. Lee and I must have looked forlorn indeed, for he promptly handed it back. "This one," said he with a smile, "is on the house."

His kindness put me in mind of an incident connected with my brother's marriage a few years earlier. At the end of that ceremony, the priest, a stranger to us, was handed an envelope containing twenty-five dollars, two tens and a five. Somehow the tens got stuck together and the priest, on looking in, assumed the total to be fifteen. This discovery brought a sneer to his lips and the remark that "Twenty is the usual donation." I'll never forget the foxy expression on Edward's face as, reaching into the envelope, he separated the two tens and pocketed the five. "Now," he said, "you have the usual donation."

There seems to be something about getting hitched that revives the boy in the man. At any rate, as Rex and I were leaving the St. Louis Cathedral after our nuptials, I noticed a milkman making his morning rounds and was seized with a yen for some chocolate milk. Our first argument took place at the church door, following which, having bought the milk, I sat on the street curb gulping it down while Rex, heels tapping, waited for me a block away.

I would hear about this one for years to come. Nor would Rex let me forget my behavior enroute to Chicago by train. Suddenly overwhelmed by memories of the hometown toward which we were heading, I took to drinking in a dedicated fashion. Before leaving St. Louis I had wired our parents. My folks and Rex's, who had come to Chicago from Indiana, were at the station to meet us, and the old-fashioned Irish party that ensued completed my slide into liquid oblivion.

***

In Chicago, my job with the American Bondholders Protective Committee was to install the accounting system for the entities under the Committee's control and audit the various resident accountants. Where each of the properties was concerned, our modus operandi was to persuade the bondholders to deposit their bonds with us for cancellation. We then issued them stock in a new corporation. By this procedure we could obtain from a bank a reorganization loan. With these funds we paid off legal fees, refurbished the property, and -- most important of all -- got some competent management into the operation.

My responsibilities were onerous and I soon found myself doing a lot of work after business hours. One night Dayton Keith, the wealthy up-state Illinois banker who headed the Committee, stepped into the room where I was laboring and invited me into his office for a chat. I made haste to complete my work, anticipating a commendation from him for the long hours I was putting in. Instead I got a friendly dressing-down. Overtime, said Mr. Keith, was a "necessary evil" to be resorted to only under abnormal circumstances. If I could not complete my duties in the allotted time, I was either incompetent or I needed more help. Thereafter I continued to toil after hours, but I saw to it that Mr. Keith did not catch me.

Once a month I visited all of our properties, without advance warning, checked the books, and counted the cash. Finding one manager with his hand in the till, I fell for his hard-luck story and instead of sacking him told him to make up the shortage. Only some fifty dollars was involved and my forbearance left me feeling very Christian-like. Unhappily, when I returned to perform the audit again, the manager's shortage had risen to six hundred dollars and I was forced to confess my error to Dayton Keith. This time his dressing-down was not so friendly; I came as close as I ever would to being fired from a job.

Once, during my months with the American Bondholders Protective Committee, I lucked into a bit of moonlighting. A Michigan Avenue eye doctor with a clientele straight out of Who's Who in the Theater told my brother that, though his practice was enormous, he was having trouble meeting his bills. Edward suggested that he employ me to examine his books. The books turned out to be in a state of chaos and impossible to audit, but I finally tracked down a stock account in a brokerage firm where the two old ladies who had been running Doc's office for many years were trying to get rich with Doc's money. Under threat of exposure and arrest, the old ladies quietly departed. I then hired a registered nurse who did the work of both, and within a month Doc was plunking money into the bank. Over the years the old ladies had relieved him of several hundred thousand dollars, and my recollection is that I charged him fifty for my services.

It is a measure of the education I got while working for the

Bondholders Protective Committee that in time I learned that the doctor I had saved from his predatory employees was himself guilty of a little skirting of the law. He was given to being open-handed in providing his theatrical clients with prescriptions for addictive drugs. He was also very vain. His work involved considerable surgery and he refused to wear glasses even though he came close to being blind.

***

Prior to my leaving St. Louis, the Committee had given me a choice: I could continue working at the Roosevelt Hotel there or I could work directly for the committee in Chicago. My choice of Chicago was emotionally satisfying but economically unwise. Though in Chicago my salary, $175 a month, remained the same, I no longer enjoyed the "perks" that had been mine in St. Louis - - free room and board, for example. More to the point, I was now a married man with heavier expenses. For a time, Rex and I had a hard scrabble of it -- but we had each other and that was enough. Rex got a job. That helped, and after a spell in a small furnished apartment we managed, by blowing the whole of my life savings, to obtain a much better place and fill it with our own things.

***

Among the properties held by the Committee was a hospital on Chicago's South Side, and it was the auditor there who informed me that he was applying for a position with the Federal Bureau of Investigation and suggested I do the same. At first I hesitated, aware that though I had done well in my classes at De Paul University I was not the holder of a degree. Still, the thought of becoming part of the FBI was compelling. This was in the late 1930s and the organization J. Edgar Hoover had put together was at the zenith of its fame as a crime-fighting body. Only a few years before, the country's most notorious bank robber, John

Dillinger, had been tracked down and killed by FBI agents on the streets of Chicago. Telling myself that I had nothing to lose, I applied -- and to my surprise was almost at once invited to appear at the local offices for an interview and an examination.

At Chicago headquarters I first took the written examination and was then directed to the office of Mickey Ladd, the agent in charge there, later assistant director at the "Seat of Government," as FBI folks called the national headquarters in Washington, D.C. As I stepped into Ladd's office, he was on the telephone. On hanging up, he told me the call was from a man at the Great Northern Hotel who had information concerning a stolen car. Handing me a slip of paper containing the man's name, he asked me to go to the hotel and interview him. As I sensed that this was part of the test, I was temporarily nonplussed on reaching the Great Northern to find that the individual whose name I'd been given was not registered there. Fortunately, I had sense enough to have him paged and, sure enough, there he was, waiting for me in the lobby. I interviewed him -- a little nervously, I daresay, for I assumed him to be an FBI agent who would report his impressions of me. On my return to headquarters, Ladd called in a stenographer and asked me to dictate the results of my talk with the informant. Using the few notes I had taken, I did the best I could. Apparently I did well enough --or perhaps I had made a good impression, for that, as I would learn later, plays a larger role in the sizing-up of an applicant than does his mark on the written examination.

In a few weeks I received a letter offering me an appointment as a special agent of the FBI at $3,200 a year. Some of my joy was diluted by the warning that this arrangement was confidential. Were I to reveal it, the offer would be terminated. So there I was, jumping inside like a schoolboy at the prospect of becoming a G-man, but unable to share the good news with anyone.

As I learned later, other fellows named to the FBI at this same time found this confidentiality a source of irritation.   My subsequent longtime friend Robert Kennedy (not the late brother of the president) was one of them.   On the train bearing him to the national capital, Kennedy encountered an old acquaintance. Naturally each asked the other where he was headed, and as both were new FBI appointees, both lied -- only to find themselves together during the swearing-in ceremony on the fifth floor of the Department of Justice building at Washington's Tenth Street and Pennsylvania Avenue, N.W.

It was there, on January 10, 1938, that I reported for duty, to find myself in a class of about thirty-eight men, most of them in their early twenties.   First we were sworn in.   Then came a lecture, informing us that the swearing-in was tentative.   Whether we became agents or not depended on how we measured up -- mentally, morally, and physically -- during the training period that lay ahead.   I winced when the lecturer gleefully spouted statistics showing the numbers of individuals who "busted out" of each class for physical deficiencies alone.

The first phase of an extensive physical examination followed.   It was conducted, as all such procedures were in my FBI days, by a medical unit of the Navy, and I got the impression that the young fellow in charge enjoyed the nervousness all of us exhibited as he outlined the tests we were to undergo and the importance of keeping ourselves fit and trim.   It was at this point that I learned that if you wished to stay in the FBI you had to watch your weight.   Whenever excess pounds appeared, you would be ordered to lose them by a certain date -- or else.

I recall the young man telling us that one of the impending exercises would consist of jumping up and down on a three-foot stool by way of measuring endurance.   To get ready for that one, three of the other agents and I practiced on a bathroom commode, jumping up and down and feeling one another's heart beats after every ten leaps.   When the day for this test came, all of us expected to flunk. It didn't help to be told by our sadistic supervisor that if any of us fainted, to think nothing of it as "that sort of thing was all in the head." His statement put the idea in our heads and, sure enough, some members of the class did faint. My recollection is that we lost only one man from the class as a result of this and other strenuous drills. Not bad, all things considered. Following that first physical examination I was a nervous wreck until the results of it were announced many weeks later.

A highlight of our opening class was the issuance to each of us of a briefcase containing, among other things, a variety of books to be studied. That evening, rummaging among the contents of the case, I found a .38 caliber automatic with a belt holster. It was only then that it dawned on me that this job might not be all fun and games. I would carry that revolver throughout my FBI career and on occasion tuck a second weapon into my watch pocket. This was a .25 caliber automatic. My reasoning was that if someone deprived me of the .38 automatic, I might get a second chance with this much smaller gun.

During that opening class, the members sized one another up and worked out arrangements for sharing apartments, a list of which was provided to us. I teamed up with Kennedy, Bob Flynn, and Jack Gleason, starting friendships that would endure far into the future. Under a deal with the Plaza Hotel in the Capitol Hill section of Washington, we got two rooms and four beds for ninety dollars a month, only $22.50 each. This was a pretty good arrangement because, as the only married man of the four, I had to send money home.

***

Rex was pregnant that year, and my roommates walked the floor with me as the great day drew near. It was a walk of some duration since Rex had a tough delivery. At last, however, on

February 6, 1938, the wire came, telling me that I was the father
of a girl whom we named Patricia after my father. I would not
lay eyes on her until she was almost four months old, and I
remember complaining to my friends that "This is a hell of a
note" -- but then, as I will have occasion to observe in more detail
later, life in the FBI had its sharp edges.

For sixteen weeks the training ground on -- fourteen of them in
Washington, the others at Quantico, the United States Marine
Corps base in Virginia, some fifty miles down the Potomac River
from the nation's capital.

In Washington, classes ran from nine in the morning until ten at
night, save on Sundays when we began at one so as to allow time
for church. Examinations were frequent and the passing grade
was eighty-five. It was endless, gruelling study. Confining too;
I do not remember a time when I didn't crack the books until
midnight. The only relief was a daily hour in the gym, without
which most of us would have gone stir crazy.

When we shifted to Quantico toward the close of the training
period, the hours began at six in the morning and were largely
devoted to firearms practice on the range. We had to qualify in
the use of the Springfield .30, the Thompson submachine gun, the
shotgun, the pistol, and an apparatus for the propelling of tear gas
that entailed a kick of such proportions that every shot yielded a
bruise on the shoulder.

The only weapon that gave me some trouble was the pistol. At
the qualifying round with that weapon you began by standing
sixty yards from a silhouetted target with a holstered loaded gun
and forty-five rounds in your pocket. At a given signal you ran
ten yards and fired from a prone position, five shots with the right
hand and five with the left from behind a barricade. After this
you ran first to the twenty-five yard line and repeated the process,
and then to the ten-yard line where you fired ten shots from the

hip. As with all our examinations, the passing grade was eighty-five. You dared not miss many hits. As the entire exercise had to be done in five minutes, you had to allow yourself a fair amount of time at sixty and fifty yards and hurry things up at the closer distances. At sixty yards, a .38 caliber shot drops about twenty-four inches. You have to aim high at that distance, and then calculatedly lower as you approach the target. I flunked the first try, but on the second (or third, I forget which) I made it -- with a sigh of relief, for this was the last real hurdle. Its passage meant that soon I would be a G-man for real.

The final step was to sweat it out until you received the assignment to your first post. Each of us was given a form on which to specify the three places he would like to be. No one, however, took this seriously. It was common knowledge that the FBI seldom sent a new agent where he wanted to go. Where the powers-in-charge did send you depended largely on what they had learned about you during the training period. Men from the South, for example -- especially those who were still fighting the War Between the States -- were sent to New York or to some other far-up-North location. As for the Chicago-born Irish Catholic named Robert E. Lee, I was sent -- you've probably already guessed it -- to that bastion of the Old South, Richmond, Virginia!

Bob Lee, Special Agent, in the early 1940s.

4

SPECIAL AGENT

By April 1938, when I arrived in the Old Dominion, my formal training as a special agent was behind me, but it was in that pleasantly slumberous little city on the banks of the James River that my education into the quirks and qualities of the Federal Bureau of Investigation (FBI) really began.

The FBI had a missionary zeal. The lawlessness of the 1930s demanded our best efforts. Now, at the end of this century, people take the FBI for granted, or even still scorn it for the crimes collectively known as "Watergate." But at the beginning, the FBI was embraced by our citizens because they were tired of living in fear, exposed to the whim and danger of organized crime and the anarchy of lawlessness that encased so many of our cities. As a result, we understood the importance of our mission, and we were filled with an enthusiasm of purpose that fired our waking hours.

The organization was so small -- some six hundred agents, nationally -- that to belong to it was to belong to a family. Frankly, the FBI became a second family to me, and many of the friendships I made there held solid through the rest of my life. I can't say that every agent knew every other agent. But I can say that practically every agent knew something about you and you about him. So, my arrival in Richmond was in the nature of a homecoming. All seven of the agents stationed there were at the railroad station to give me a warm welcome and to help me find living quarters pending the arrival of Rex and the little daughter I had not yet seen.

***

Family life, of course, has its dark as well as its bright sides, and in the years ahead I would have many occasions to appreciate and many occasions to fret at the degree to which the official life of an FBI agent dictates his social life. The tight security under which we labored and the long hours put in precluded much activity outside of the group. There was no time for making friends or for pursuing interests unconnected with our work. Our poor wives! Theirs was a lonely and a narrow world. All they had was each other.

For example, I recall an agent at Richmond who happened to be one of the Bureau's few certified public accountants. He had four children and he objected to doing overtime on the grounds that in a few hours he could accomplish more than any of us younger fellows could do in a day. He was right, but when efficiency rating time came around he was judged, like the rest of us, not alone on the quality of his work, but also on the quantity of the time spent at it. His eventual resignation to go into private practice was his family's gain and the Bureau's loss.

Myron Gurnea, my boss at Richmond -- the Agent in Charge, to use his proper title -- was one of the great gunmen of the FBI of my day. During the beginning years of the Bureau, its agents were not specifically authorized to bear arms. Most of them carried private weapons, but generally speaking the corps of agents was not notable for its marksmanship.

The organized gangs of criminals spawned by the coming of

Prohibition highlighted this deficiency. The members of these illegal syndicates were exasperatingly mobile, easily putting themselves beyond local control by fleeing to some other parts of the country. As crime became Federal in nature, the Federal government was obliged to step in. Soon laws were being passed giving the United States Department of Justice and the FBI jurisdiction over a growing variety of heinous crimes. This action led to legislation requiring FBI agents to carry arms and to be trained in their use.

At the time I joined the FBI this authorization was only a few years old and many agents still lacked the high-grade marksmanship the changing crime scene demanded. To rectify this situation, Director Hoover had the country scoured for crack gunners. About twelve in all had been found. The "flying squad," we called them. Once the rank and file of us had zeroed in on the location of a criminal -- the status of a John Dillinger, say -- the flying squad was called on to make the apprehension. Recruited from the San Francisco, California, Police Department, Gurnea belonged to this outfit -- a tall man, well over six feet, lean and rangy, with the sort of eyes one thinks of as looking right through you. Officially he was the head of our Richmond office, but as I soon realized this post was simply where the FBI parked him between the special assignments that sent him elsewhere almost constantly during my Richmond days. I remember following his exploits in the press and wishing I were with him -- but at that time I was far from ready for such enterprises.

At my first efficiency rating he puffed me up by calling me the "most promising young agent" he had yet encountered -- and then deflated me by observing that my "personal appearance" left something to be desired. I couldn't argue with him. I was so broke supporting myself and my family in Chicago that buying clothes was a problem. But I was determined to win Gurnea's approval, and when Rex and my four-months-old daughter Pat finally arrived I greeted them in a newly-purchased suit.

***

Our first living quarters consisted of one room with kitchen privileges in a home overrun with vermin. Little Pat's crib was mis-routed and for several weeks her bed was a pillow in a dresser drawer. We were overjoyed when in time we found a one room apartment that, though terribly hot, was clean and comfortable. Here from time to time we entertained, with little Pat sleeping peacefully in the same room with the festivities.

Some of my time in Richmond was spent among that city's prostitutes. FBI jurisdiction over prostitution rested on the White Slave Act of 1910, popularly known as the Mann Act after its sponsor, Congressman James Robert Mann of Illinois. Forbidding the transportation of women for immoral purposes from one state to another, the Mann Act has proved useful in getting at otherwise elusive criminals, even as John Dillinger's transportation of stolen cars across state boundaries brought that lawbreaker under Federal jurisdiction and the Federal tax code permitted the trial and conviction of Al Capone.

I no longer remember exactly when I began keeping an eye on a house of prostitution run by a madam named Belle Hodges. I assume that a complaint about the place came in, and I remember my conclusion, following a routine investigation, that if I snooped about long enough I could find that at least one of Belle Hodges' girls had been brought to Richmond from outside the state of Virginia. Were that guess to prove correct, a raid on the premises and an interrogation of its occupants would be in order.

My first step was to comb the local police records. There I found that Belle Hodges had been picked up on occasion but as far as I could determine she had never spent a night in jail. I did not give the local police a clear idea of what I was looking for.

Madam could be paying them off, and they might let her know what I was up to. If payoffs are being made in this sort of situation, the one thing the locals fear is Federal involvement. Madam wouldn't care whether she was hit by the locals or the feds. If she got hooked on a Federal rap, she might squeal on her local protectors, much to their embarrassment. In the Belle Hodges case there must have been no payoffs at a high level. In the subsequent raid the Richmond police were not only included but were also notified hours in advance, and no tipoff occurred.

Finding little help in the police files, I began a detailed surveillance of Belle's place. That it was a house of prostitution was clear from the beginning. The size and nature of the traffic in and out could be explained in no other way. Actually it was not a house. It was an apartment, a suite of rooms above an optical store.

I remember the trepidation with which I took the proprietor of the store into my confidence and arranged to use his place to watch the comings and goings connected with the establishment above. After all, he could have been a satisfied customer and tipped Madam off. Apparently he wasn't. At any rate, he didn't.

I spent many weeks in the optical shop, frequently obtaining the license numbers of the cars driven by Madam's customers. Some of these I had traced. On occasion I ascertained the addresses myself by following the customers to their homes. Some of them were pillars of Richmond society. The local press could have had a field day had I released their names. But I wasn't out to embarrass Madam's clientele, only to determine whether or not her operation came under FBI jurisdiction.

Eventually, in an effort to get a fuller view of how the house worked, I called on Belle Hodges. She proved to be a very pleasant person, a prostitute, well into her forties, still pretty in the face but taking on weight -- who had the good sense and

sufficient smarts to move into the proprietorial end of the only
business she understood. I called on her two other times and
enjoyed her wit and personality. I think she also enjoyed mine.
In any event, she treated me with respect, possibly because that is
how I treated her.

One of the things an FBI agent learns early in his career is that
when dealing with prostitutes he must keep his guard up and his
mind on higher things. Any prostitute feeling that a lawman is
closing in on her is going to try tripping him up by claiming that
he has made a pass at her. So commonplace is this charge that
often when an FBI agent must talk to a prostitute another agent
tags along, or, if that is impractical, stations himself where he can
observe the interview. I had no choice but to visit Belle Hodges
on my own, but from first to last I went out of my way to keep
the relationship platonic, and as soon as a conference ended I
made haste to record in writing whatever had been said.

Through Madam I made the acquaintance of several of her girls
and picked up some information on them. Most of them were the
products of underprivileged homes. I never met one from
Wellesley. I soon learned not to ask "How did a girl like you
ever get into a place like this?" That, the girls told me, was the
question nearly every new patron put to them. I heard some
pathetic tales and at the risk of being called a sentimental slob I
have to admit that I believed them. More to the point, probes by
the FBI showed them to be accurate. Most had grown up in
extreme poverty and with little prospect of marriage. Drunken
and abusive parents figured in their recollections. Girls brought
up on farms recalled giving themselves to a traveling salesman in
return for a little fun, only to realize in time that their favors
could be exchanged for money. After that came the move into a
city and usually the taking on of a pimp. Between sharing their
proceeds with the pimp and the madam, all of those I met were
broke. All looked far older than they were, and all yearned for a
different life. Several of them, I discovered, had found husbands,

and I was given to understand that by and large these marriages had turned out well.

Every day, during my surveillance of Belle's place, I went through her trash. It was, while engaged in this chore one morning, that (forgive the pun) I struck pay dirt: a one-way railway ticket for a girl who had come from Raleigh, North Carolina, to work for Madam. Here was evidence that a Federal law had been broken. I lost no time in presenting it to my boss, Myron Gurnea, suggesting that we move in on the place and arrest Madam and her girls. At first he was skeptical. "A relatively small house of prostitution," he said in effect. "Isn't that the sort of thing the local gendarmes should be handling?"

I showered him with arguments to the contrary. I urged him to examine the notes I had taken on my conversations with Madam and her ladies -- notes showing that they had connections with some of the big-time criminal types in the Richmond area. Conceivably, the opportunity to interrogate the lot of them would reveal information useful to the FBI. At the very least, I argued, a raid on Belle's place would point to the existence in the South of an interstate white slave ring whose exposure would earn us some nice headlines.

Although later Gurnea accused me of having done a "snow job" on him, he bowed to my request, quickly obtaining the necessary clearance from headquarters in Washington and the dispatch from there to Richmond of a few super sleuths to help us with the big raid.

Our preparations for it were comprehensive. I provided data to one of our cartographers. He used it in the drafting of detailed street maps of the vicinity of the house. These maps became the base for briefings of the raiding squad. Each member of it was given a particular assignment. Every possible mishap was considered and prepared for. If one of the raiders were shot, for example, one of his buddies had the phone number of the ambulance in his pocket and was under orders to use it at once.

As it was my case, I rode to the street door of the house alongside Myron Gurnea. My surveillance had established that at a certain hour every night food was delivered to the house. Our plan was to go in by the front door when that happened, simultaneously issuing a signal for other officers to enter by the back door and windows.

When at the usual hour the waiter showed up with a tray of food, Gurnea and I followed him up the stairs. When the door was opened, we promptly stepped past him, guns drawn, and announced that the joint was being pinched. Meanwhile, other members of the raiding party were coming up the back stairs and crawling through the windows. In a matter of minutes, the customers had been separated from the girls and were being questioned to make certain that none of them was involved in the operation of the house. Even as this interrogation was going on, a couple of new patrons appeared at the door. Both were ushered in protesting that they were at the wrong address. Both were questioned and then, along with the others, allowed to depart.

While these interviews were being conducted, I was given the task of riding herd on the girls in a separate room. What a time they gave me. They made nasty jokes. They invited me to bed, pointing out that if I would only "loosen up" I could have a very good time. Great was my relief when the girls were removed to the FBI offices and subjected to a night of grilling, after which they were carried to Norfolk, Virginia, which had the only suitable place in the area for the incarceration of women apprehended under Federal law. At Norfolk, as I recall, they were held for a few days as material witnesses.

Meanwhile, the necessary indictment having been procured, arrangements were made to take Belle Hodges to Federal Court.

There she received a probationary sentence and the judge delivered a lecture to the effect that cases of this sort belonged in police court. By this time Gurnea had come to the same conclusion. Not me. I thought the enterprise worth the bother. For one thing, it had the effect of closing down, for a time at least, whatever houses of prostitution Richmond had. For another, it provided me with several good informants that I found useful in other cases. One thing I remember with a touch of sadness is Belle Hodges coming up to me after her trial. "Thank you for your courtesies," she said, and then walked out of my life. I was to miss her; once a sentimentalist -- well, I'll leave it to you to finish that sentence.

***

Juvenile delinquents absorbed a good deal of my time in Richmond. Teenage boys would steal cars in Washington, D.C., and head south. If they were picked up in Virginia, the interstate angle was established and the local police turned them over to us. First offenders did not go to jail but the convictions that went on the public record would haunt them for life. When I showed up wherever they were incarcerated, I saw evidence that some of them had been maltreated by the police, who in those days were not much concerned with the rights of prisoners.

Speaking of police brutality, I never saw even the slightest sign of it on the part of my colleagues in the FBI during my years with that outfit. I always made sure the kids I was assigned to had been properly fed and supplied with cigarettes. Frequently, they would ask me what they should do about the predicaments in which they found themselves. I was tempted to advise them to get in touch with their homes and a lawyer. But as the job of an FBI agent is to catch the malefactor and leave his prosecution to others, I could not offer such counsel. All I could do was urge them to tell the truth. Unfortunately, once a youngster had supplied me with a signed statement of guilt, it was difficult for him later to enter a plea of not guilty. One lad, however, did just that and in the end he was declared innocent. I remember this case well because the prosecutor, the then United States attorney in Richmond, was Sterling Hutcheson, later a Federal judge. A true southern gentleman was Hutcheson. He took the time after the trial to tell me that the important thing in law is not to win every case but to serve the ends of justice by doing one's duty. These days I sometimes reflect on how important it is that the investigator of a suspect never become his prosecutor as well. Any investigator worthy of his salt is moved by a conviction that the person he is after is guilty and that, no matter what the court says to the contrary, the evidence of guilt is there somewhere.

The waywardness of the young and who or what is to blame for it -- on these subjects millions of words find their way into print yearly. Having worked for a time with juvenile offenders, I subscribe to the old-fashioned notion that how kids turn out depends on how intelligently and diligently their parents guide them. I'm grateful for having grown up in a home where at least one parent was always on hand and neither parent had any compunction about telling us youngsters how to behave. These days television gets much of the blame. It wasn't around in my day. Had it been, I'm sure my parents would have lost no time telling us what we could and could not watch and seeing to it that we followed instructions. No doubt we would have hated them for it -- but as can be said of priests and ministers and rabbis, the main job of a parent is not to be popular.

Someone is always decrying the increase in juvenile crime. But is the crime growing all that much or is it simply our counting of it that is growing? When in the early part of the twentieth century my policeman father found a kid in trouble he took him to his parents by the scruff of the neck. Often that ended the matter. Today he would have to book the youngster and fill out a mess of forms. These would have to be correlated in Washington and publicly released. All this stems from an act passed by Congress in 1934, making the FBI the central reporting repository for crime statistics and burdening the Bureau with the task of persuading law-enforcement units the country over to submit their data on crime to the FBI. As more and more local bodies joined this program, the figures on crime escalated-making it possible for the FBI director to issue a yearly press release decrying the increase in law-breaking and pressuring the Congress to provide the Bureau with more money to fight it.

How the regulations covering the handling of stolen cars distort the figures is a case in point. Every enforcement unit is required to put a price tag on every vehicle it recovers. If the car involved has been driven by a thief over a state line, the local police turn it over to the FBI. Before doing so, however, they put a price tag on the car and when the car reaches the FBI another price tag is put on it. If you add up the credits thus taken for stolen cars, you end up with a figure close to the value of all the automobiles in the United States. Both the local units and the FBI use the figures obtained in this manner to swell their requests for governmental appropriations.

***

I've often wondered about the FBI official who assigned me to Richmond. Did he keep sufficient track of things to see how the people of that city reacted to Robert E. Lee? If so, he enjoyed some chuckles. I can remember a few newly-made acquaintances taking me to a bank in Richmond to examine documents connected to an account once kept there by the celebrated general. On occasion I would give out that I was indeed a descendant. That never worked. The denizens of Richmond knew too much about the great man. Sooner or later their knowledgeable questions tripped me up and the truth emerged.

The Richmond press loved to put my name in print. Everything I did, even a trip to a local police office to question a youngster who had driven a stolen car across a state line, got into the papers. Where FBI activity in Richmond was concerned, I was soon getting more attention locally than Director Hoover. I realized that this would never do. Whatever J. Edgar's virtues, modesty was not among them. I was not in the least surprised when in the summer of 1938 I received orders transferring me to Newark, New Jersey. Before I could get there, however, a letter from Hoover directed me to report to Washington, D.C., for a special assignment. Rex and the baby made this change with me, and as the special job lasted three months and carried extra pay, a per diem of six dollars, we lived it up in the national capital as we never had in Richmond.

My job in Washington was to assist a highly capable agent and certified public accountant named Nate Franklin in an audit of the Alien Property Bureau created in the first World War to take custody of properties confiscated from hundreds of thousands of German aliens during 1918-1919, the years of America's participation in that conflict. By 1938 many of these properties had been reclaimed, but not all. The purpose of the audit was to inventory the remaining properties so that the affairs of the bureau could be wound up and the bureau itself abolished. I don't have to tell you that these plans did not materialize. Thanks to the activities of one Adolf Hitler in the late 1930s, the bureau was kept alive to serve the country again during the second World War.

The properties still held by it in 1938 ranged from ships to rare coins and included extremely valuable items, certain patents and copyrights, for example. The property that regularly made the headlines was that of Grover Cleveland Bergdahl, widely regarded as World War I's premier draft dodger. My recollection is that at the commencement of the conflict Bergdahl gave out that he was a conscientious objector and was seized by the military. While being transported from one camp to another he escaped and made his way to Germany, taking with him a large sum of money. By

1938, alarmed at Hitler's activities, he had returned to the United States and surrendered as a fugitive. He received a minor sentence and as far as I know lived out his life somewhere in Pennsylvania, quite comfortably, on the money we had guarded for him during his exile.

One of my last memories of the audit of the Alien Property Bureau is that its chief officer, the custodian, whose name escapes me, was found to have been traveling to his out-of-Washington home at government expense. He had either resigned under duress or was about to when I moved on to Newark.

***

A number of interesting new acquaintances awaited me there. Among them was the agent in charge, Alvin Paul Kitchin, soon to become a Democratic congressman from North Carolina and one of the finest bosses I ever had. Another was Carmine Bellino, a certified public accountant destined to win fame later as chief investigator for the Senate Rackets Committee whose chief counsel, Robert F. Kennedy, carried on a vendetta against Teamsters boss Jimmy Hoffa that ultimately resulted in Hoffa's sentence to a Federal prison. Still another new acquaintance was a tough old guy named Abe Dickstein. Agent Dickstein was the funniest man I ever met. His specialties were imitations of the top bad men of his era, Hitler and Mussolini. J. Edgar Hoover once summoned Dickstein to the office maintained by the director in New York and commanded him to be funny. The funny thing to all of us was that without further ado Dickstein went into one of his bad-man routines and soon had the head of the FBI in stitches.

He was not amusing to the big New Jersey gangsters on whom he focused the bulk of his attention. He knew who they were and was relentless in his pursuit of them. I remember one in particular, a smoothie named Longies Zwillman. Again and again,

Abe would invite Longies to his office and Longies would come, lawyer at his side, and answer questions. Abe never got Longies but he did develop an operation that had the effect of enabling us to bring other notorious hoodlums to book. For this operation, a gang of us -- I remember going on one of these forays -- would descend on Atlantic City, New Jersey. There we would round up a batch of the local criminals and question them in a hotel room. What made this procedure helpful to us was that prior to assembling our assorted no-goods we got a court order empowering us to interrogate them under oath. Then, if we found untruths in their statements, we could arrest them for perjury. For law-enforcement people this can be a very useful device. After all, Alger Hiss was not tried for the traitorous acts which he committed, but for perjuring himself in a court of law.

Mayor Frank Hague of Jersey City, New Jersey, was a constant irritant. He will be remembered as one of the last of the big city bosses. When Norman Thomas, American Socialist leader and perennial candidate for the presidency, came to Jersey City, Hague's police force literally picked him up and deposited him in nearby New York. Of course there were complaints, mostly from the left wing. Of course we looked into them -- tongue in cheek. And of course nothing came of our efforts.

***

Thanks to my background in accountancy, I was assigned to numerous cases dealing with bankruptcy. These were not happy experiences. At that time, and this may still be the case, the laws covering bankruptcy were so ineptly written that even after you had laboriously gathered all of the available data proving your case, it was like pinning jelly to the wall. In Newark, New York City, and Philadelphia, a group of individuals, using different names, would open businesses, run up a mountain of debt, and then take bankruptcy. By the time the FBI got into the matter, no one could find the records, and in those instances where the facts could be reconstructed, no one but the agent involved would understand them and the United States attorney was understandably reluctant to prosecute. In the rare instance when you got a conviction, the defendant suffered a heart attack in the closing moments of the trial and the judge, moved by this drama, would put him on probation. In my days I watched many a teenage boy jailed for stealing a car and more than one financial manipulator sentenced to eighteen months on probation for stealing millions. To be privy to a crime of this size but unable to do much about it can be frustrating. I recall thinking that there ought to be a law requiring every business to maintain adequate books. With the pertinent information readily available, showing that false statements have been transmitted through the mails for credit purposes could be a snap.

A number of embezzlement cases also came my way. As a rule, after I had completed one of these, the president of the bank would call me in to say thanks and to ask what internal controls should be strengthened to prevent a recurrence of the crime. Before long, I was giving every executive the same answer. "No controls can prevent a crook from snitching, but you might reduce the possibility of it by paying your employees a living wage." Often, the guilty party was trying to provide for a growing family or to meet the demands of a greedy wife on pitifully low wages.

Consider, for example, the case of a young man -- we'll call him Leonard -- who was struggling to maintain his family (three children and another about to arrive) on a trifling salary. When the bank's only vice president retired, the people in charge thought well enough of Leonard to shove him into that post. But there was no immediate increase in salary. Leonard was informed that he would have to wait until a retired president died and was removed from the pension arrangement he had made with the bank.

But Leonard couldn't wait. Presently he was asking his boss for a loan of five hundred dollars to help pay the medical expenses for his new baby. The boss's response was a lecture about "living within your means, my boy," and Leonard, desperate, dipped into the till. He began by taking five hundred dollars, but by the time I was called in he had got himself into the clutches of local gamblers and owed the bank eighteen thousand dollars.

I had the sad duty of serving the warrant of arrest. What a scene: the children screaming, the wife, baby in arms, clinging to her husband as I cuffed him. Back at the FBI offices I told my boss that I wasn't equipped to play the meanie and might as well resign. He talked me out of it, noting that if I thought there were mitigating circumstances in this case I could cite them in my official reports.

I went beyond that action. I talked with the judge and had the pleasure of hearing his honor, as he pronounced sentence, blast banks in general and Leonard's institution in particular for their penurious treatment of employees. Leonard was put on probation and was profuse in his thanks to me, and I stayed on the job.

As a rule, the embezzler is intent to invest whatever he takes, pick up a little profit for himself in this way, and then put the money back. It would be interesting to know how many of our respected fellow citizens have gotten away with just such undertakings.

In this connection, I remember a curious case that for me began with a call from a bank in Morristown, New Jersey. One of the bank's officers was "acting strangely." That was about the extent of the complaint and I hastened to Morristown, knowing that delay can be fatal in these matters. Should the records be destroyed or the suspect flee, I would soon be on the carpet trying to explain why I hadn't got to the site of the trouble faster.

What I discovered, after a few days of poking around, was a scheme so commonplace and simple that I couldn't understand why its perpetrator -- let's call him Harry -- hadn't been suspected long since. Every bank has some dormant trust accounts. Alert auditors keep their eyes on these, figuring that a person bent on lifting money is most likely to do this from inactive accounts. Harry was hitting some of these dormant accounts. At the end of each month he plugged in a comparatively small figure to make things add up. To do this he had to go through hundreds and perhaps thousands of checks that had cleared the bank until he found one bearing exactly the figure needed. He then listed this check as outstanding on the bank's statement in an effort to foil examiners.

They shouldn't have been fooled for a minute. For twenty years the bank's accounts had been audited by a well-known English firm. Obviously its auditors did not make it a practice to verify outstanding checks. Had they done so, Harry's taking ways would have come to light twenty years earlier.

The most interesting angle of this case was that at the time I came into it, Harry's investment of his stolen funds was paying off well. When I confronted him with such data as I had uncovered, he blithely admitted helping himself to the money and offered to make restitution. I recall traveling around the state with him opening up the various safety deposit boxes and mail drops he had established. Then we went to the officers of the bank and Harry paid back every dime he had taken, some twenty thousand dollars. He then pleaded guilty, received a suspended sentence, and moved to Hackensack, New Jersey, where he used the money he had left -- thanks to shrewd investments of his ill-gotten gains -- to buy himself a bowling alley. The bank sued him for his profits, but I can't give you the outcome of this novel venture because, by the time it materialized, I was no longer in New Jersey.

**

It was in New Jersey that I had my only extended brush with

antitrust work. In this area the FBI is under the control of the United States Department of Justice. Only under direct orders from the Attorney General can the Bureau initiate investigations into price-fixing and other suspected violations of the antitrust laws.

My one experience in this field left me convinced -- and subsequent observations have borne out my foreboding -- that these laws tend to be the tool of politicians. Over the years I've noticed that whenever the national government shifts from Republican to Democratic or vice versa, the incoming sachems use the antitrust laws to go after a few scalps. Nine times out of ten the only result is more government intervention in business.

One case I was assigned the Department of Justice established a squad of lawyers and accountants, about a hundred of us, to probe the fertilizer industry. Then, getting together, we arranged for a series of simultaneous raids on fertilizer firms the country over. At exactly ten o'clock on a Monday morning one or more of us invaded the offices of a firm, demanding its books and records for examination. We carried no subpoenas, and many of us thought this rather highhanded treatment of legitimate businessmen. But orders are orders and we carried them out, albeit shamefacedly.

The major activity was in New York, where my assignment was to an outfit known as the Tennessee Corporation. When I explained my mission, the officers of the company reacted as I expect officers of all of the raided organizations did. They called in their lawyers who, after hours of chatter, handed me a list of questions, including one asking under what section of the Constitution I was proceeding. I took these to the attorneys for the Department of Justice at the Federal Court House in New York. Then we waited, knowing that in time the Tennessee Corporation, having meanwhile removed anything bordering on the suspicious from its records, would let me eye its books -- preferring a man at its offices to responding to a subpoena requiring the transfer of a truckload of files to the Court House.

So matters worked out; I spent a month reading correspondence and minutes of directors' meetings. I learned a lot about the business, including the happy knowledge that if we ever run out of enough land, we can grow large amounts of food in water and in ultraviolet light. I enjoyed these perusals but nothing came of them. Indeed nothing came of the investigation of the fertilizer industry anywhere in the country. There were no indictments and, so far as I can recall, no cases were so much as presented to a grand jury. And with a hundred of us on the job, the Lord only knows how much that operation cost.

Are such boondoggles inevitable in a national government as mammoth as ours? I'm afraid so. Perhaps a clause should be added to Murphy's Law, to wit: that when a government is given enough money to burn, somebody is going to find a way of burning it.

I was never comfortable in Newark. Neither was Rex. Both of us rejoiced when toward the end of 1938 orders came through transferring me to the city of our memories and our dreams -- Chicago.

5

DETECTIVE

During my two-year tour of duty in Chicago I at last found myself doing the things that I joined the FBI in the hopes of doing. To my delight William Devereaux, the agent in charge, did not limit me to investigations calling for a background in accountancy. He also put me on the trail of criminals high on our list of wanted persons. As I didn't intend for "the boss," as we called Devereaux, to think I expected to be treated any other way, I never asked him why he gave me these interesting jobs. But I could guess. He knew about my father. By January of 1939 when I started work in Chicago, Pat Lee had retired from the police force and was functioning as a private detective for the Chicago Transit Company, operator of the overhead railroad line known throughout the area as the L. He was still a very popular man on the force, however, and time after time the mere mention of his name opened doors for me to information and other assistance only the local constabulary could provide.

Like my experiences in Richmond, those in Chicago contributed much to my understanding of how the FBI operates. Few readers have to be told that such statements as "The Mounties always get their man" are exaggerations. Detective work isn't that foolproof. Neither is it that glamorous. Much of what an FBI agent does can be described as drudgery. He must follow up every lead, even those that from the start strike him as probably leading nowhere. This can take months, even years of labor, and no matter how well he does it he doesn't necessarily get his man.

What does happen frequently is what scientists call serendipity, the accidental discovery of something important, but altogether different from what you set out to uncover. Very often, while not finding the crook you're seeking, you stumble onto information that leads to the capture of some equally malign do-badder.

Early in my FBI days I encountered a situation of this sort. Not only did I not find my man, I have reason to believe that his whereabouts remain a question mark to this day. But in the course of not finding him, I inadvertently developed data that led to the arrest of at least two big-shot criminals and provided me and the Chicago FBI office with a great deal of useful information.

This case originated in Los Angeles, California, during the stickup of a large branch of the Bank of America. What happened, as we learned from a teletype, was that three men invaded the place, corralled customers and employees in a corner, and ransacked the premises. A feature of the escapade was the use by bank robbers for the first time of a radio receiver tuned into local police calls. Word coming over this gadget that a heist was in progress at a certain site gave the bandits the few minutes they needed to abscond with a goodly sum of money.

What interested us were the teletype revelations that the theft had been planned in Chicago and that a fingerprint found on the counter of the bank in Los Angeles had been identified as belonging to one Morris Kessler, a small-time bum living on Chicago's Near North Side. Kessler's mother was the proprietor of a drinking place on Blue Island Avenue in that area, a filthy joint patronized by human scum, as several of us learned on paying the place a visit. Looking back, I can say that our call on

Mrs. Kessler at that time was premature. Had we simply staked out her barroom and waited till her son came to see her, we might have nabbed him. As it was we gave her time to warn him and she did exactly that. All this I ascertained much later. During that first visit to her dingy hole-in-the-wall, all she told us was that she hadn't set eyes on her son for several weeks.

At this point I took over. My strategy was to gain Mrs. Kessler's confidence by spending a great deal of time chatting with her at her Blue Island Avenue establishment. She was a hard-bitten old lady, but in the weeks that followed I came to feel a certain fondness for her, even a degree of respect. I guess there's some good in the worst of us and if you spend time enough with a person you begin to understand why that person has turned out as he or she has. If Mrs Kessler lacked the ability to rise above her circumstances, well -- thus she was built. A cat can't help it because it cannot swim. It's not necessarily a coward because it sits on the bank and lets another cat drown.

In my eagerness to get her to see things as I saw them, I resorted to every low-lived trick in the book. Among other things, I pretended to be Jewish. That seemed to please her. Why, I can't say, since judging from the behavior she permitted in her groggery she knew little or nothing about her religion -- a fact that made it easy for me, who knew even less, to fool her. Little by little, I convinced her that her "Moishe," as she called her son, would be safer in our hands than if he remained at large. After all the two men with him in the Los Angeles robbery were by now well aware that his identity was known. They were also aware that were we to grab him, he would try to get a mitigation of his punishment by squealing on them. I remember the day this fact dawned on Mrs. Kessler.

I remember saying to her, "As things stand, those two fellows" -- his partners in crime -- "have a strong interest in Moishe's demise." And I remember her replying, "I see what you mean."

It was then she revealed what I had long suspected, that following our premature visit to her Blue Island Avenue barroom she had warned Moishe to stay away. She swore she had not seen him since and was ignorant of his whereabouts. I conveyed these data to my office but I did not identify the source of them. To have done so would have made Mrs. Kessler an accessory to the crime and I figured that the FBI should concentrate on locating her son and not waste time prosecuting his mother.

Once Mrs. Kessler came over to our side she helped us in every way she could. She allowed me to look at such belongings as her son had left with her, and among these I came upon a notebook in which Moishe had listed approximately a hundred names. Checking these out kept me busy for some time. First I ran them through the files at police headquarters in Chicago and through those at the FBI in Washington. Practically all of them were known to the law-enforcement authorities. Many, to be sure, were petty punks, but a few turned out to be criminals summa <u>cum laude</u>. Several had been tried on murder charges. One had been acquitted of such charges on three different occasions. In each instance he pleaded self-defense, and, given the way things are in the underworld, my guess is that all three pleas were justified. Members of gangs hold human life cheap. For them, murder is simply a tool of their trade, to be used as needed, and, if they are squeamish about doing the act themselves, they hire a professional "hit man" to do it for them. Convictions in cases of hoodlums wiping out hoodlums are few, possibly because there's nobody to root for in the courtroom, the individual killed being as much a menace to society as the killer.

Thanks to the clues turned up in my investigation of the names in Kessler's notebook, I uncovered the identity of one of his girlfriends, whom I'll speak of here as Brenda. For a time before approaching her I kept her under surveillance, hoping that she would lead me to Moishe.

She was a tall blond, very good looking in a brittle way. I learned quickly that she was on intimate terms with a number of gangland types. She carried a gun in her purse and often acted as front girl in cases involving the planning of a stickup or break-in. From time to time, for example, she would pose as a customer at a fur shop, gathering enough material over a spate of visits to provide the potential thieves with a useful pencil sketch of the premises. She was a mercenary lady and thought nothing of taking money for exposing the whereabouts of her boyfriends to members of a rival gang. No less than two of her one-time lovers were gunned down in her presence. In both cases she had put the finger on them. When at last I met her and revealed who I was, I lost no time in giving her to understand that I knew of these betrayals. In this manner I made sure that she would try no monkey business on me. After all, one word to the gangland types that she was an informer and she would have been fitted at once for a concrete slab.

The night on which I finally picked her up was a fiasco from beginning to end. My guardian angel must have been on hand. Otherwise, I could have been fired or transferred to some FBI Siberia for a series of mistakes, the thought of which makes me shiver to this day.

Having had Brenda under surveillance for several weeks, I put an eavesdropping device in her room at a Near North Side hotel. Simultaneously, another agent, Norm (Steve) Stevens, and I ensconced ourselves in a room across from hers. From here we were listening to what was going on in her room when along about midnight she received a male visitor. Morris Kessler? Steve and I had no way of knowing but judging from what Moishe's mother had told me about her son, I thought this could be him. At this point we should have called our office and got some advice on how to proceed. Instead, excited by the possibilities confronting us, we decided to handle the situation on our own.

What a mistake that turned out to be. We did not have Kessler's fingerprint with us. We did have what is called its classification code, information which we took to mean that none of Moishe's fingerprints contained whorls, the name given to one of the patterns common to fingerprints. We reasoned that once we got hold of our suspect, we could simply examine his fingers. Should we find a whorl on any of them, we would know that we did not have Kessler. If we found whorls, we would be justified in taking him to the office.

So our strategy stood when, soon after the man's arrival, he and Brenda left the hotel to make the rounds of the local bars. Steve and I followed, becoming more convinced with every drink we enjoyed that we were looking at Morris Kessler. When he and Brenda returned to her room, we decided to grab him when he departed.

This was about 3:00 A.M., and when shortly thereafter the man left to get some food, Steve and I stopped him on the street. There we questioned him briefly. We also ascertained that his fingertips were a mass of whorls, meaning, according to our present understanding, that he was not Morris Kessler. When we let him go he hastened back to Brenda's room. By this time another girl had appeared there and over our listening device we heard him tell the two of them about his encounter with Steve and me, adding that he must take off now "because I am hot."

That word "hot" put Steve and me in a stew. It occurred to us that this man might be someone in whom the local police were interested. Adding to our dismay was the sudden realization on Steve's part that we had misread the fingerprint classification code, that Morris Kessler's prints, far from being free of whorls, consisted of nothing but whorls. Panic-stricken at the likelihood that we had let our man slip, we crossed the hall, kicked Brenda's door open, and seized him. Not without difficulty; as we well knew he was unarmed but the girls put up an awful fight, in the course of which one of them flushed something down the toilet.

All this happened about 5:00 A.M. Having nabbed the man, we called in our boss and some other agents to help us interrogate him. Our suspect protested his innocence of any wrongdoing as we undressed him, and sure enough he did not have certain marks known to be on Kessler's body. At that point Steve and I decided to take his fingerprints and check them out at the police station. Having obtained the prints we asked him to sign on the card on which they had been impressed. Never will I forget the stricken look on his face as he wrote his name and said, "Well, I guess the jig is up." I couldn't very well ask him what jig since I had to pretend that I and my fellow agent knew what we were doing. Imagine our relief on learning shortly thereafter that the name he signed belonged to one of the most wanted fugitives in the FBI files -- a man who only a week earlier had held up a gambling saloon in Kentucky and with his partner had made off with $20,000 in small bills. If the fellow we caught so accidentally that night is still around and happens to read these words, he will learn that had he signed his card with a fake name we would have released him within the hour.

***

Fortunately for Steve and me, our boss did not report our mishaps to Washington. Instead of a reprimand I received a letter of commendation.

Now I had another case on my hands -- tracking down the man with whom our captured fugitive had held up the gambling saloon in Kentucky. His name was Marvin Pickett and he was wanted not only for the Kentucky holdup but also for the killing of a cop in Richmond, Virginia. Again I followed the ancient procedure known as <u>cherchez la femme</u> -- find the woman, find the girlfriend of the fellow you're seeking.

Her name, I learned in due time, was Sue Cassidy and she was living in Chicago. Another agent and I put her under surveillance for a time. Then one night we picked her up. She had spent the evening at a variety of bars in a mobster-dominated section of the North Side. She was both drunk and tough. We had our hands full getting her to the office, and once there, we had to chase her all over the place while she threw things at us. Eventually she quieted down, and after getting enough identification from her I let her go on her promise to return and talk to me the next day.

To my surprise she did return and was penitent on learning that she had manhandled Federal officers. For some reason the very thought of the Federal government always seems to put the fear of God into the average small-time hoodlum. This one, I could tell, needed a drink, so I bought her one at a fancy lounge. It always amazed me how these mob-connected types warmed up when you treated them nicely. I guess the tactics I used on Sue Cassidy can be likened to those of a lobbyist. I wined and dined her and thus got her confidence. Within a few days she had helped me lay hands on Marvin Pickett. Her cooperation did not come free, of course. She had to be paid. Today, thinking of the generous sums I handed to my informants in my FBI years, I wonder how many of such payments were ever reported to the Internal Revenue Service.

One day Sue informed me that she had heard from Pickett. He was in town and had arranged to meet her that evening at a pub on North Clark Street. For that evening's work I rounded up half a dozen crack agents and plenty of artillery, for Pickett was reputed to be a tough customer. That night the owner of the pub Sue had named must have wondered whence his enlarged business came. The other agents and I arrived early and stayed until closing time. We gave the single girls in the place a big play while waiting for a man who never appeared.

I was crushed, but my faith in Sue Cassidy remained strong.

When, on getting in touch with her, she asserted that she had no idea why Pickett hadn't shown, I believed her. As she had reason to think he was still in town, I decided to look for him the hard way. Obtaining a map of the Near North Side, I circled the gang-infested area where he was most likely to be. Then I got a list of all the transient hotels in the area. it was a long list but I set out to hit all of them if it took me a month. This, to be sure, is not efficient detective work. To pursue every criminal in this manner would require the presence in a big city of more lawmen than civilians. But my fellow agents had teased me about Pickett's failure to appear at the North Clark Street pub, and I was determined to get him.

All I had to work with was a photograph of him, and such was the nature of the neighborhood that even if someone recognized him, he or she might not choose to admit it. From hotel to hotel I trudged, simultaneously flashing the photo of Pickett and my FBI badge carrying a picture of myself. More than once -- and this had happened to me before and would happen again -- the person to whom I showed photo and badge would shake his head at the photo and then, pointing to the badge, add, "But I've seen this fellow around."

On the third day I lucked out. A bellboy identified the person in the photo of Pickett as a guest at his hotel. He also informed me that on the very night of our futile wait for Pickett at the North Clark Street bar he had been in an automobile accident -- a revelation that confirmed my faith in Sue Cassidy.

The bellboy gave me Pickett's room number and I called my office, saying that I thought it unwise to wait, that I was going to get him at once, and asking that help be dispatched in a hurry. Then I went into the room, gun drawn, only to find it unoccupied, to my great disappointment -- and equally great relief.

Soon my boss showed up, having posted a couple of agents in the lobby. When soon thereafter we heard a key in the door, we placed ourselves in front of it, weapons at the ready. In stepped a maid, bringing linen. There was a scream. The sheets she'd been carrying flapped in the air and she scurried down the hall with me behind, pushing money into her hand and urging her to keep quiet about what she had seen.

After my return to Pickett's room, the boss and I began a systematic search of the place. An old suitcase yielded what we were seeking, the loot seized by Pickett and his partner in the Kentucky saloon holdup. Incidentally, $20,000 in small bills makes an impressive pile. When, shortly after our discovery, Pickett turned up we took him without trouble and a few days later he and his partner were enroute to Kentucky to face prosecution.

Among the names on the list in Morris Kessler's notebook was an "Archie" whom I came to suspect of being one of the bandits involved with Kessler in the stickup of the Bank of America branch in Los Angeles. On learning that Archie was an habitual criminal, currently confined in the Illinois penitentiary at Joliet, not far from Chicago, I began paying him regular visits.

Archie's future was bleak. He had been arrested so often that the chances of his ever going free were minimal. Consequently, he tended to be cooperative in the hope that I might be able to get some sort of break for him. I made it clear that there was little I could do other than advise the state authorities of his assistance. That, I pointed out, might be of some help if and when a parole board sat on his case. I brought him small gifts and left a little money for him at the cashier's cage, and in time he opened up.

He never said anything that could link him to the Los Angeles robbery, but he admitted knowing Kessler. His story was that Kessler's partners in the Los Angeles crime had indeed caught up with him and that his body, heavily weighted, now lay at the bottom of a lake in Wisconsin.

This lead, like all others, was followed up. The FBI saw to it that the lake was dragged. No body was found but I was able to verify enough of the story to lend some credence to it. People living in the area of the lake remembered seeing strange men with a boat at an isolated cabin along the shore. They remembered seeing these individuals at about the right time and getting the impression that they hailed from Chicago.

And on that uncertain note, I must end the story of the search for Moishe. To the best of my knowledge, that's where it stands to this day.

***

Kessler was but one of the fugitives I took after during my FBI days in Chicago. In most instances, I was pretty lucky. Either the crook was in the hands of the law by the time I moved on to a different locale or another agent, building on the information I had developed, was able to complete the job.

Of the many absorbing chores assigned to me in Chicago, the ones I most enjoyed involved so-called "con men." The confidence man is an interesting study. For one thing, he's always likeable. He has to be. Personableness is one of the elements that must be on hand if the con man is to bring off his often amazing deceits. The other necessary element is the presence in the victim of a high degree of greed. Indeed, the victim has to be almost as indifferent to breaking the law as is his victimizer.

I smile at the recollection of a case where the person conned was every bit as larcenous as the person who conned him. This case began one morning when I was invited by a gentleman of such generous proportions that I think of him as "Big Boy." He was a prosperous truck dealer and his reason for calling on me was to see if I could track down a man named "H" who had talked him out of $5,000. Big Boy was trying to lease trucks to branches of the Federal government and "H" claimed to have influence inside the bailiwick of the United States attorney in Chicago.

"Naturally," he told Big Boy, you'll have to sprinkle a little money around among certain people in the U.S. attorney's offices." It was to take care of this that "H" requested and got the $5,000. Amusing to me was Big Boy's revelation that he had accompanied "H" to the offices of the U.S. attorney and had waited in the lobby while "H" went inside to make "the necessary arrangements."

Having listened to this tale, I had no choice but to present Big Boy with a couple of obvious conclusions. One was that he had been swindled out of $5,000. The other was that had he actually "sprinkled money" around as suggested, he might have found himself facing a charge of attempted bribery. I know from the expression on Big Boy's face that my words came as a surprise to him. Never for a moment had it occurred to him that he was doing anything remotely illegal.

To complete this little story: Within a few days "H" was found and taken into custody. He turned out to be a delightful fellow, humorous and intelligent and completely free of the crudity and meanness of spirit common to habitual criminals. He blithely admitted everything, and when I asked him about that visit with Big Boy to the U.S. attorney's offices, he said, "Oh, that's an old ploy. I didn't talk to anybody. I spent some time in the men's room. Then I returned to my victim and assured him that everything was all right.

6

THE FBI AT WAR

The story of the FBI in wartime needs to be told, and this chapter is merely one attempt at what should be a larger study. Heroism on the home-front is often forgotten, but the men and women in the FBI were instrumental to the success of the allies' victories in Europe and in the Pacific.

The year 1940, my first as a special agent in Chicago, followed shortly after the outbreak of the second World War in Europe -- a cataclysm that compelled the Federal Bureau of Investigation to direct more and more of its energies to the problems of national defense. Granted, the United States was not a participant in the struggle. "Not yet," I remember some of my fellow agents saying in the tone of men convinced -- correctly, as we now know -- that sooner or later we would be drawn in. With its large German population, Chicago was a hotbed of pro-Nazi and anti-Semitic movements. Legal as these activities were in peacetime, we had no choice but to start compiling lists of those who should be arrested or at any rate kept under surveillance if our country entered the conflict.

In 1940, we were not well prepared for this shift of emphasis. It took us some time to get geared up, but in the end we did a good job. Not once, during that long and terrible war, was there an incident of enemy-instigated sabotage within the confines of the United States.

Personally, I'm inclined to credit J. Edgar Hoover with this triumph. Since his death in 1972, the founder of the FBI has been the subject of considerable criticism. Some of it may be justified, much of it surely is not. I do know that much of it is based on innuendo and hearsay, and the so-called "facts" are often very questionable. I do concede that we were zealous -- but I saw no evidence that we were zealots. Rather, I believe that Hoover and the FBI were effective because they were dedicated to both the country and its laws. Like any organization, the FBI is composed of individuals, and these individuals do make mistakes. They also make judgment calls. It makes more sense to remember that constant vilification of our institutions is as reactionary as blind faith in them. As a nation, we need a more balanced, informed, and seasoned view of the FBI.

I know that we owe Director Hoover much more thanks than he gets these days. Now we look at him as a strange, power-hungry monster. Some people accuse him of bizarre, kinky behavior. It's easy to slander the dead. In my experience he was nothing but a dedicated public servant and a gentleman. He knew how Washington worked, and he found a common language of power. But, in my view, he didn't abuse his authority. However, I know that the country is stronger and safer because someone of Hoover's intelligence and commitment occupied the Director's chair. It's a big position to fill, and few are able to run the FBI effectively. We have witnessed the difficulty since Mr. Hoover's demise. While not taking anything away from those who followed, I still believe that he was tailor-made to be Director.

By the 1940s, thanks to his skills as an organizer and as a public relations man, Mr. Hoover had created in the public mind a respect for the FBI that left that body free to do its work without the well-intentioned but often disastrous assistance of civilian vigilante groups. It's worth noting that this situation had changed by the 1950s when Communism replaced Nazism as the enemy. Perhaps by then faith in the FBI had somewhat diminished or the emergence of another large intelligence operation, the Central Intelligence Agency, had confused the issue. At any rate the war against Communism in the United States was marred by the frequent establishment of anti-Communist groups by civilians whose penchant for careless name-calling injured the very cause they were attempting to further.

***

In 1940 so-called bunds, active pro-German organizations, were cropping up all over Chicago. All were holding regular meetings and the members of some were marching about in uniforms similar to those worn by soldiers of Adolf Hitler. Most made their headquarters in taverns or beer gardens, and soon we were haunting these places, picking up whatever leads we could. Once in a while the adherents of a bund caught onto us and unpleasant words passed, although so far as I can recall no violence occurred.

Among the data obtained in this manner was the revelation that most of the bunds were putting their money in a certain bank on Chicago's North Side. Naturally we began at once seeking ways of gaining access to these accounts so as to identify the individuals responsible for them. To procure such a list would be to have in our hands the names of many of the country's leading pro-Nazis, potential spies whenever America joined the hostilities. We worked hard at this search, and one day an incredibly good break gave us the access to the records of the bank that we needed.

It started with a phone call from the treasurer of the bank, a call to the FBI office that happened to be transferred to me. The treasurer's report was that a cashier had disappeared with some $40,000 in cash. Needless to say, I lost no time in getting to the bank to gather the details. This was on a Monday and what I learned, on reaching the bank, was that the embezzlement had taken place on the preceding Saturday. The vanished cashier was a young fellow whom I'll refer to here as "Fred." Efficient and well-liked, Fred had been with the institution for some seven years. Saturday morning he had left his cage long enough to purchase a bag of groceries. On returning, he removed the groceries and emptied the contents of his cash drawer into the bag. The guard on duty at the time remembered him as nodding a polite goodbye at closing time, and not until Monday morning were the theft and the disappearance of its perpetrator discovered.

An examination of Fred's personnel file yielded useful information, including the whereabouts of his apartment and the names of his friends in the bank. He had a girl there and naturally the old admonition, cherchez la femme, occurred to me. It occurred to the bank authorities too, and when they hired a Professor Kelly and his lie detector to check her out I was annoyed at some of the questions put to her. Among other things, the professor wanted to know if she and Fred had sexual relations. I recall telling him that this was not pertinent to the case and, as it turned out, the young lady had no connection whatever with the theft.

After perusing the files, I hastened to Fred's apartment only to discover that it had been abandoned. From neighbors I learned that Fred lived with his mother. She too had gone and the revelation that she was an invalid suggested pressing medical bills as a possible motive for the foolish thing her son had done. A careful search of the premises yielded, among other facts, that Fred was the owner of a dog. "Ah ha!" I recall muttering to myself. "This could be a case, not of cherchez la femme but of cherchez le chien." Assuming that Fred had boarded his pet somewhere, I put flyers out to hundreds of kennels in the area, and within a few days we had located the animal in Rochester, Minnesota. Simultaneously we learned that Fred had brought his mother to the Mayo Clinic there for a series of tests. We, of course, put the kennel under close watch and when some ten days later Fred showed up, we nabbed him.

It was a pathetic case. As we pieced the story together, it became clear that Fred's mother was forever harassing him to make more money to provide her with medical help that, according to the tests at the clinic, she did not need. From the clinic, Fred had taken her to the home of relatives and then had returned to pick up his dog. He had paid his mother's bills at the clinic, purchased a car and a set of golf clubs -- but a substantial portion of the embezzled funds was intact and I like to think that eventually he would have given himself up. Thanks to the recovery of most of the money, the bonding company involved was happy and Fred received a suspended sentence. I liked him. I sensed that overpowering circumstances had impelled him to his rash act. I helped find him another job and off and on during the remainder of my FBI days in Chicago he dropped by to talk things over with me.

Human greed is a sly motivator of much human action. The aftermath of Fred's case provides an example. It was a standing practice of the bonding company to give a 15 percent reward for the recovery of money and in Fred's case they offered this to me. When I pointed out what they already knew -- that FBI agents cannot accept such rewards -- they offered to sell me the car that Fred had bought for a nominal sum. This too I declined. Then they suggested something to the effect that they had a secondhand set of golf clubs on hand -- meaning the ones Fred had bought -- and that if I would not take them, what could I do if I woke up on Christmas morning, then only a few weeks in the future, and found them leaning against my door? My reply took the form of a question: How in the world would I know where they had come from? Chuckles all around and I supposed they had got the message. So, Christmas morning I hurried to the door, dreaming of spending some upcoming day on the links, wielding my ill-gotten clubs. They were not there.

***

Still, my success in tracking down Fred and arranging for the
return of most of the cash he'd embezzled did not go unrewarded.
To the owners of the bank I was such a hero that they allowed me
to study the accounts of those customers who were contributing
to one of the local bunds or to any other agency of Hitler's
Germany. It was in the course of this inspection that I discovered
that a number of checks were going to the Third Reich for the
purchase of German bonds called Reichwunder Marks.   The
significance of these securities was that subscribers to them could
not cash them unless they came to Germany within a stated
number of years. Here was a clue to just which Americans were
so enamored of the Third Reich that they were planning to move
to Germany after that nation had accomplished what appeared to
be its objective, namely the conquest of the world. It was clear
that the purchase of Reichwunder Marks was not limited to the
customers of one Chicago bank. Here, clearly, was a world-wide
undertaking and what the FBI needed was a list of all the
subscribers, or at any rate of all of those living in the United
States.

By dint of great patience and work I discovered that the secretary
of the organization selling the bonds was a native of Germany,
now living and working as a printer in Chicago. I also learned
that he was the sole occupant of an apartment in a building on the
North Side.

Did he keep a list of the subscribers to the Reichwunder Marks on
the premises? Would it be feasible for me to break in and have
a look? As America was still at peace with Germany, I had no
legal grounds for such an action. Obviously I could not request
authorization for it from the FBI. Just as obviously, if I broke in
on my own and got caught, the FBI would have no choice but to

dismiss me on the spot. More to the point, the evidence in the apartment, if there were any, would then disappear.

Having considered these matters carefully for at least one minute, I decided to take the risk. Nor did I have any trouble persuading one of my fellow agents, Ed Dixon, to join me in the enterprise.

Legal purists will say that Ed and I were violating the very laws we were sworn to enforce. I couldn't agree more; but, mind you, although our country was not then at war with the Third Reich, it was clear to many of us that it was going to be in the near future. When that time came, a knowledge of what Americans were active and effective supporters of Nazism would be information of great value to the defenders of our national security.

For several days Ed and I kept the printer's living quarters under close observation. We watched the printer himself, as he came and went, acquainting ourselves with his appearance and routines. We learned that he worked by day. We concluded that we would be safe in breaking in after he left the apartment in the morning.

His flat was on the first floor and so positioned that its front window overlooked the steps up to the main entrance of the apartment house. We walked nonchalantly into the hallway from the street and jimmied the printer's door open. It was wintertime. Once inside the apartment we removed our outer garments and began a leisurely search of the place. Within an hour we had located a three-by-five inch filing cabinet containing the names and addresses of persons all over the United States. We had also located the printer's passport and I was reading it when, glancing toward the front window, I saw our subject coming up the steps. "So much for the luck of the Irish!" I muttered to myself. Apparently we had inadvertently picked on the printer's day off from work. Visions of being sacked by the FBI flashed through my head as I grabbed my hat and overcoat and began a dash down the corridor of the building -- only to realize with a jolt that the printer had reached his apartment and that my fellow agent, Ed Dixon, was still in there.

Back I ran, convinced that all was lost. I couldn't have been more wrong. Far from panicking, as I had, my associate had begun to question the German printer in a stern and peremptory manner -- and the German was giving every evidence of being scared to death. Perhaps because of the authoritarian creed to which he adhered, he was simply unaware that to get rid of us he had only to call for the police. Grasping the situation, I joined Ed in the questioning and presently we were taking the printer and his three-by-five filing-card cabinet to the FBI offices. There, further grilling brought out that the names on the cards were indeed those of the American subscribers to the Reichwunder Marks. We completed the evening's festivities by photo-stating all of the cards and then letting our frightened German depart with his set.

I have forgotten how we explained our seizure of the list to the FBI bigwigs. Whatever we said was accepted, and for several weeks after the United States entered the war the list Ed Dixon and I had uncovered was one of the major sources used to conduct a series of raids over the country.

Practically all of the individuals on our list were picked up and placed in detention pending processing. Aware that many of the persons thus seized could be innocent dupes of Nazi propaganda, the officers in charge expedited these procedures as much as possible. As fast as a detainee's innocence could be determined he was released.

I credit this timely strike at possible spies for the absence of internal sabotage by the enemy during the conflict, and to this day I regard my illegal break into the home of a German printer as my major contribution to the war effort. Indeed, I was guilty of such break-ins in connection with other cases where national security was at stake. I do not apologize for these, but I hasten to add that in run-of-the-mill criminal cases I never stooped to such behavior. It was a time of war, and extraordinary measures were needed.

***

Today some of the cloak-and-dagger activities in Chicago during the months before our country's entry into the war appear downright childish. But at the FBI, tracking our potential enemies down was serious business. One morning a tall, good-looking, outdoorish type of man came into the FBI offices, saying he had some information to impart. He was working as a groom for a wealthy family living on Chicago's exclusive North Shore Drive. His report was that his boss, one of the city's V.I.P.s, had organized a small bund. Its members met weekly in a large barn on the family estate, drilled in uniform for several hours, and had taken on the names of various Nazi leaders, such as Hitler, Goering, et al.

Though I found this tale hard to believe, I had to spend several days running it down. Thanks to careful surveillance and help from the police, I was able to verify it. Our rich V.I.P. turned out to be behind most of the anti-Semitic instances in the city. He was hiring hoodlums to smash the windows of Jewish-owned shops and paint scurrilous signs wherever possible. Whenever one of his hirelings got arrested, he was quick to appear with a bondsman and a lawyer.

As we were still at peace with Germany, all we could do was keep an eye on the troublemaker until he made the mistake of neglecting to register for the draft. Whereupon we had him indicted, and during the trial which ensued he came into the courtroom in clerical garb and claimed clerical immunity. He received the maximum sentence for draft-dodging: ten years.

***

Months before the bombing by Japan on December 7, 1941, of the American naval base at Pearl Harbor, Hawaii, pushed our country into the second World War, the FBI was struggling to get a line on the Japanese intelligence activities in the United States. My own efforts in this area took a decided turn for the better when sometime in the early months of 1941 I made the acquaintance of a petite and pretty young woman who was a "Nisei," which is to say a second-generation Japanese-American. I remember her name vividly but, on the chance that she may still be around, I shall refer to her here as "Miss J."

She was in a perfect position to give me information about those Japanese government officials who, enroute to Washington, D.C., stopped off at Chicago to have a little fun and take in the sights. Actually she did not give me the information, I paid for it -- a retainer of fifty dollars a month; and as I had to advance this sum from my own pocket and as my expense reports were honored slowly, I often had to borrow to keep my attractive informant on the payroll. I remember touching my boss on occasion and of assuring him that I was going to get everything there was to be got out of Miss J if it took the last dime he had.

Over the years "Miss J" had established herself as a guide for the Japanese government officials spending time in Chicago. She steered them to the best night clubs and procured white women for them. There was something about her that inspired confidence and the visiting big shots often talked over their plans with her. She in turn advised them on how to operate when they got to Washington and sometimes provided them with contacts there. Naturally she was able to give me a great deal of useful data.

Why did she provide this service for the FBI? I wasn't sure. She could have been a double agent, but I strongly believe that she was working for us and us alone. I never caught her in a lie or in any action that could be called detrimental to the United States.

To facilitate our collaboration, I rented a modest office for her in the building where the Chicago FBI maintained its headquarters. Here, and sometimes elsewhere, I interviewed her concerning Japanese activities in the United States. She typed reams of material for me. This I put into report form, distributing copies to all FBI offices and to other interested law-enforcement units. She kept me posted on what Japanese officials were coming to town and what their purposes were. Frequently these visitors left messages to be passed on to subsequent visitors. These I had photo-stated and sent immediately to Washington. I never knew how important they were as they were written in Japanese and translated at the seat of government.

Among the many officials who stopped from time to time in Chicago was Itizi Sugita, head of Japanese intelligence. One of his first actions on reaching the city was to ask "Miss J" to help him procure internal newsletters and bulletins from as many American military installations as possible. These he dispatched to Japan where you can be sure trained observers, studying them with care, found among the bits and pieces of gossip in them much information about the movement of American troops.

Sugita also asked "Miss J" to get him detailed maps of Pearl Harbor. When she informed me of this request, I told her to utilize whatever commercial sources there were. Naturally she turned to the famous map-makers, Rand/McNally, and when that they were unable to supply what she had in mind, the company itself contacted the Chamber of Commerce in Hawaii. From this unlikely source, Sugita obtained a large number of maps, some of them ten feet square. These showed the Pearl Harbor area in complete detail and included information on the varying water depths and other characteristics of the harbor. Obviously Sugita was spying, but since we were still not at war with Japan all I could do was keep an eye on him.

When I told "Miss J" that I wanted to search his room on the tenth floor of a North Side hotel, she obtained for me the combination to the lock on a case filled with documents that he kept in his room. She then dropped a key to me and took Sugita on a two-hour shopping trip. During this interval another agent and I inspected the room. Once in there, we rigged up an orange crate with four electric light bulbs and mounted a recomar camera on the top, focussing it on the bottom so that we could quickly photograph the documents kept in the locked case. These we sent to the seat of government, totally ignorant of what they revealed, of course, as they were written in Japanese.

One day "Miss J" called from one of the Chicago railroad stations to tell me that she had custody of the bags of a Japanese special ambassador then enroute to Washington for talks at the highest governmental levels. This offer was too much for me. I told her to get the bags back. By the time this happened, I was convinced that war with Japan was coming and I didn't want the responsibility of having started it.

Even before our entry into the conflict on December 8, 1941, "Miss J's" usefulness had attracted the attention of the Bureau's big shots and they decided that she could be even more valuable in New York. After she left Chicago, I would see her only once again, and this after I had been shifted to Washington where we enjoyed a pleasant talk. The Bureau had set her up in comfortable circumstances and my recollection is that she stayed in New York throughout the war and performed valuable work.

***

After her departure I turned again to pro-Nazi activities. An amazing incident connected with these labors began when I received a phone call ordering me to pack a bag and report to the FBI offices. I was given to understand that a job had come up which would keep me away from home for a week or so. Accordingly, I kissed Rex and our babies -- a second child, Robert

Edward, having arrived on August 1, 1939 -- and took off. My instructions were to take a certain room at the Palmer House in downtown Chicago and keep an eye on a German spy just come to town from the British crown colony of Hong Kong, where she was known to have been in close touch with the Nazi apparatus functioning in that part of the world.

My room at the Palmer House was across the hall from hers. Some other agents and I were directed to keep her under observation at all times. As she moved about in the erratic manner of a person accustomed to being shadowed. Our task was a difficult one. Eventually, however, we succeeded in tracing her to an antique shop that turned out to be the headquarters for one of the numerous pro-Nazi rings operating in Chicago.

It so happened that one of my co-workers on this mission was a good-looking young agent who spoke German fluently. Our job became considerably easier when one day this young man followed our German spy onto a sightseeing bus and made a point of sitting down beside her. Within minutes a boy-meets-girl-and-you-know-what relationship had developed. Soon agent and spy were going out together, a situation which made life easier for the other "shadowers" and me. She was an attractive young woman but, knowing that his movements were always under scrutiny, the young agent manfully limited himself to an occasional session of hand-holding. Then one night, after the two of them had spent some hours on the town, she invited him into her apartment. I promptly got up on a table and peeked over the transom. Sneaky behavior, yes, but my orders were never to let her out of sight. The scene below was riotous. She was coming on to him madly and he was painfully resisting, not because he didn't want her but because he knew that Lee was looking through the transom.

***

Pleasant as those FBI years in Chicago were, they were marked by one period of tribulation. Sometime in the late fall of 1940, my mother collapsed in the bathroom of our old North Side house. The doctor, summoned at once, diagnosed a stroke and almost total paralysis. Mother's condition necessitated around-the-clock nursing.   None of us had ample incomes and I remember a conference in the basement -- Father, Edward, and I -- during which each of us agreed to contribute a certain sum every month to foot the bills.   We braced ourselves for a long siege of staggering costs -- but, thoughtful as ever, Mother relieved us of these burdens by dying within a few weeks. It was the last of her many gifts to us.

On December 12, 1940, the day of her death, all of the members of the immediate family were on hand. At the end we were all in the room with her, all on our knees -- my sisters, my brother, my father, the priest who had come to give Mother the last rites. The doctor too. When he told us she was gone I swear that I saw the shadow of a cross taking form on the wall. Probably I was seeing what I wanted to see. I said nothing of this to the others, fearful that if I did they would haul me off to the nearest booby hatch.

***

So enjoyable was my FBI work in Chicago that I recall on occasion muttering a little prayer to myself, "Dear Lord, do let me stay here forever." I knew that couldn't be. The FBI doesn't work that way.   Sure enough, one day Bill Devereaux, the boss, informed me that Washington, D.C., was calling. It seemed that in some of my efficiency ratings described me as "possessed of administrative ability." Just what the seat of government was looking for, he said. I resisted the move with all the power at my command.   For one thing, I wasn't interested in exercising whatever administrative ability I had. For another, in those days the government did not pay for the moving of household goods and the transportation of wife and dependents. For still another, I shared the general feeling of agents out in the field that the seat of government was a cold, dull place, overburdened with brass and unduly concerned with rules and regulations. But, having borrowed five hundred dollars to finance the journey, I found myself, the wife, and the kids riding the Baltimore and Ohio Railroad eastward -- destination: the seat of government.

On reporting for duty at FBI headquarters in Washington, I found myself working in the office of the Chief Clerk under an Assistant Director, W. R. Richard Glavin. Eventually I moved up to a supervisory position, that of Chief Clerk in charge of fiscal matters, but prior to this promotion my major job was to assist with the recruitment drive then underway to enlarge the Bureau so that it could cope with the problems certain to arise after our country entered the war. I reviewed the investigative reports on prospective employees and either turned them down or sent them up the line to be further reviewed by Glavin or by Clyde Tolson, the main assistant to the Director.

A cherished memento from the FBI days: a signed photo from "The Director." Dated September 20, 1941, it reads: "To Mr. and Mrs. Robert E. Lee, with all good wishes. J. Edgar Hoover."

7

J. EDGAR HOOVER

At the time I reported for duty in Washington, J. Edgar Hoover's battle to free his agency from the Civil Service Commission was well underway. Already all FBI employees, except fingerprint classifiers, were exempt from the Commission's rules and regulations, and Hoover's aides, myself included, were buttonholing members of the Congress in an effort to get the change that was to make the FBI the only Federal agency completely exempt from Civil Service.

'Tis the better for it. If the FBI needed to hire another classifier under the procedures in effect when I came to headquarters, it had to ask Civil Service for a list of eligibles and hire from the top of that. Under what was known as the "rule of three," the Bureau could turn down the first two -- but that was all. Determined to disengage his agency from this hampering arrangement, Director Hoover saw to it that everyone on every list of eligibles was investigated and that case histories, showing that most of them were patently ineligible, were shown to influential members of the Congress. In due time this ploy succeeded. The Civil Service agreed to let the FBI do its own hiring in its own way. Its own firing too. It's that privilege, I'm convinced, that over the years has made the FBI one of the most efficient units of the Federal government. In my day, and I suppose this still applies, the FBI fired as large a number of employees every week as other agencies managed to fire during a whole year. In my opinion, to be sure, some of the FBI's firings were uncalled for. Most were justified, however, and the Bureau functioned the better for having jettisoned its deadwood.

I'm aware that the Civil Service System, was introduced in the late nineteenth century to protect Federal employees from the so-called spoils system, under which every change in the political coloring of the presidency meant a loss of jobs to thousands. Obviously the spoils system was wrong. Just as obviously the Civil Service System, misleadingly labelled as a "merit system," is wrong too, in that it provides little or no means by which an agency head can cleanse his department of incompetents. By the time such an administrator has taken into consideration the myriad criteria laid down by the Commission tenure, veteran's status, minority rights, and what have you -- he has learned that almost the only way he can shed a nincompoop is to kick him upstairs.

Under the various regimes of President Franklin D. Roosevelt, and especially during the second World War, the government payrolls were loaded with persons hired from outside the Civil Service System. Once on the rolls, these people were gradually blanketed into the system so that Roosevelt's successor could not get rid of them. This created a generation or two of built-in patronage. Ultimately it worked itself out through deaths and retirements, but in the interval it did a great deal of harm.

Because the FBI is not tied into the Civil Service System, it has proved notably impervious to political pressure where its hiring practices are concerned. Soon after I assumed my duties in the office of Chief Clerk, I had occasion to watch the Bureau resist an effort by politicians to use it in this area.

***

Since in the early stages of the Second World War most employees of the Bureau were deferred from the draft, we got a fair number of applications for employment at this time from persons interested primarily in avoiding military service. One day an application crossed my desk from the son of a partner in a large and prosperous Chicago law firm, with whose members I was sufficiently acquainted to know that none of them was likely to be interested in the modest remuneration of a government job. Accompanying the application were endorsements of the young applicant by a number of political figures, including some of the more powerful individuals in the United States Congress. Fearful that these well-known names might influence even J. Edgar Hoover, I called on him in person. I told him what I knew of the Chicago law firm and had the satisfaction of seeing him nod his head as I finished and of hearing him assure me that "this young man will not be employed by us."

During the early years of the Second World War, deferment from the draft applied to practically all male employees of the Bureau, including a few thousand fingerprint classifiers. It was only after the stringencies of the conflict made the classifiers subject to the draft that I realized that their deferment had not been an unmixed blessing. During those opening years of the war many of the younger fingerprint men expressed an interest in volunteering for the service on condition that they be given officers' commissions. One of my tasks was to talk them out of this. I recall handing them a song and dance to the effect that they were contributing all they could to the war effort in their present positions -- only to feel silly when the deferment of the classifiers was lifted and thousands of them found themselves being drafted sans commissions.

Nor can the special agents be said to have benefited from being exempt from the draft. The years immediately after the war saw the passage of many laws giving all kinds of benefits to veterans -- preferences that none of us agents would enjoy. Aware of this situation, President Franklin D. Roosevelt offered to blanket all agents into the armed services and give us commissions. Director Hoover turned this proposal down. He did not want the military dominating his agency. For the Bureau his decision was a correct one. On those of us who had functioned as special agents during the war it worked a hardship.

Thereafter, whenever there were reductions in force at the Bureau, we were the first to go. Without the privileges extended by law to veterans we found it difficult to get other jobs in government. All I have to show for what I consider war service is a certificate bearing the printed signature of J. Edgar Hoover and saying that I served with the FBI during the hostilities.

***

When I started my work in the office of the Chief Clerk in 1941, the Bureau had 1,596 agents. By 1946, when the recruitment drive subsided, this number had risen to 4,886. At this writing the number is about 15,000.

I don't have to tell you that the labor involved in screening and hiring over three thousand agents was intense. Never in my life have I worked as hard or for longer hours than in the office of the Chief Clerk. For us recruiters, bringing in new agents was the most important task. At the same time, however, we had to recruit the thousands of additional secretaries and file clerks that an ever-growing roster of agents made necessary.

Our employment process was costly and cumbersome. Every prospective employee, agent or clerk, was subjected to an examination covering his or her entire life to date. I remember my relief on persuading my superiors to modify this procedure where the clerks were concerned. I recall pointing out that practically every clerk was an eighteen-year-old female with a high school diploma. It followed that her background was unlikely to contain anything that might make her a threat to the FBI. Bowing to this reasoning, my bosses instigated a process under which a clerk could be put to work without a formal investigation, with the understanding that her continued employment was contingent on the results of a subsequent investigation.

To speed up the acquisition of clerks we sent a group of agents out to interview prospective employees. Those that seemed to qualify were finger-printed and sent to Washington where I funneled them into jobs unless the fingerprinting yielded a report of some impropriety in their records. For a time this procedure worked well enough, but of course there came a day of reckoning when the deferred investigations showed many of the youngsters so employed to be less than acceptable. At this point it became my job to fire them -- a most disagreeable business. For several years, I fired ten or more a day. The Bureau's standards are high and in many cases I felt like Simon Legree, but what had to be done had to be done. Many of these kids were from small towns where at the time it happened, their employment by the FBI was local news. Some had been given farewell parties, only to find themselves slinking home, unemployed, a few months later. I remember trying to make myself feel less of an ogre by telling friends that I was doing these young women a favor by getting them out of Washington.

***

Sitting behind a desk and engaged in recruiting new employees and firing others who didn't maintain the Bureau's high standards was by no means as exciting as investigative work in the field -- tracking down bank robbers or spies as in Chicago. But I did what I was assigned to do and managed to have some fun even doing dull jobs.

One assignment made me custodian of a lot of money. One of

the first things we did after the United States entered the war was to seize the Japanese and German embassies. In the Japanese embassy the raiders found only a modest amount of cash, about $20,000 as I recall. But in the German embassy they seized eight or ten mail sacks of currency, millions of dollars evidently intended to be used for espionage or sabotage. I was told to place this money in a safety deposit under my name until I received further instructions. Normally such funds as these would have been transferred to the Treasury Department. I don't know why this case was handled differently unless it may have been a means of denying the money to our allies as a fortune of war. Anyway, I didn't raise any questions. I leased a walk-in safety-deposit box in a nearby bank and the funds stayed there all through the war and into peacetime. Finally, when I was no longer employed by the Bureau, I was asked to sign a release of the money. I often thought what a waste it was for the government to leave these millions of dollars lying in a vault drawing no interest.

***

In Richmond and Newark and Chicago my fellow agents and I thought of the famous Director of the FBI as simply one of the pins on the map, showing the location of every agent, that hung behind his desk in Washington. Now, working in the office of the Chief Clerk, I came to learn a few things about J. Edgar Hoover. Mind you, I did not get close to him. With the possible exception of his right-hand man, Tolson, nobody got close to him. He saw to that.

Mr. Hoover was a fallible person, just like the rest of us. he had his faults. He was as cold and hard as they come. With one exception, General David Sarnoff of the Radio Corporation of America, he was the most conceited man I ever met. He saw to it that every agent was schooled in the art of public relations and those who excelled at this were kept busy making speeches extolling Mr. Hoover and the FBI. Members of the

Appropriations Committee of the House of Representatives will tell you that they discourage agency heads from aggrandizing themselves at the taxpayer's expense by keeping funds for public relations very low. I assume that the FBI got little money for such activities, but Hoover was adept at giving other names to the generous sums spent for such purposes. High-price talent was brought to Washington to carry out so-called investigations and studies whose real objective was to glorify the FBI and its boss. Hoover saw to it that every college graduating class in the country was talked to at least twice a year under the pretext of recruiting personnel for the Bureau.   Hundreds of newspaper editors, reporters, and commentators were regularly contacted by persons in the FBI skilled at buttering up such individuals.

It's safe to conclude that, as the old saying goes, Hoover came to believe his own press clippings. His self-absorption was intense. Take, for example, the controversy surrounding the maintenance of the cars that carried him hither and yon. If the clock on the dashboard was found to be keeping imperfect time, an assistant director was called on the carpet and a large amount of money spent in putting the gadget to rights pronto. Many a supervisor suffered a cut in salary because one of the cars was not properly dusted or a heater didn't work right. I know of one agent who was transferred from Washington because the windshield wiper on a car in which Mr. Hoover was riding failed to work in a rainstorm. Air conditioning in cars was scarce in World War II days but Mr. Hoover's vehicles had it and his chauffeur was instructed to drive around the block a few times before Mr. Hoover got into the car.

During the war years keeping the Director's cars spotless was difficult. Employees at the garages where we took them to be washed frequently waved us away, pointing out that "There's a war on" and they had more important things to do. Often some of us agents avoided trouble by washing the damn things ourselves. From the food rationing imposed on the rest of us, the

Director was exempt. His secretary saw to it that his ice box was well stocked. Perhaps she did this on her own, but my guess is that he knew and encouraged it. He certainly knew that from time to time young male employees of the FBI were used to help maintain his home.

In the years I worked near him he was fond of running up to New York City for a bit of fun. Great care had to be taken to get him a train sleeper that was not over the wheels. Regulations stipulated that government employees could be recompensed for nothing better than a lower berth. As Hoover didn't like that, his assistants talked the Congress into writing a clause into the appropriations act that permitted a train compartment for travel when the transportation of classified papers was involved and personally authorized by an agency head. Thousands of government people rode the trains with classified material every day, but so far as I ever knew J. Edgar Hoover was the only one to do so in the comfort of a compartment.

In a way, these actions are understandable in the swamp of Washington. They are not excusable, but they are understandable.

Hoover was a product of his childhood, and some background gives his foibles context. Much that puzzled me about the Director in the old days is clearer now, thanks to several recent books about Hoover. The Director was born and grew to manhood in a house on Seward Square in the Capitol Hill section of Washington, D.C. In its way the Seward Square neighborhood was as homogeneous as were the Irish Catholic enclaves of my own growing-up years. All Seward Square residents were white. Practically all were Protestant and practically all of the male bread-winners were middle-level employees of the Federal government. To Seward Squarians, home, country, and religion were the anchors of existence. For many years J. Edgar taught Sunday School, first at a Lutheran church and later at the Presbyterian church that was to be the center of his religious life thereafter. It is safe to say that he continued to be a Sunday School teacher for the remainder of his life. To him the all-white and Protestant society in which he matured was the only good society, and he watched with increasing pain the changing racial attitudes and moral values or the twentieth century and particularly the gradual disappearance from portions of American society of respect for respectability.

The only African Americans ever seen in Seward Square were those who came into the area to work as housekeepers or at other blue-collar tasks. Understandable, given this background, is Hoover's lifelong conviction that menial positions were the only ones blacks could handle. By the time I came to work at FBI's seat of government, Hoover had outgrown the simple and aesthetic comforts of his growing-up years. Quite without realizing it, I'm sure, he had become a sybarite. To provide himself with the luxuries he now craved he had surrounded himself with black menials -- a maid and five men who functioned chiefly as chauffeurs. So dependent on the services of these blacks had he become that as the Second World War developed he made all of the chauffeurs special agents in the FBI so as to prevent their being drafted into the military.

Thanks to Hoover's attitude toward African Americans, few difficulties confronted the FBI when, during the Second World War, President Roosevelt established the Fair Employment Practices Commission and authorized it to solicit reports showing how many blacks were on the payrolls of the various Federal agencies. At the time this commission was set up, the FBI could point to no more than a dozen blacks among some twelve thousand employees, and the next fifteen years saw a mad scramble by the Bureau to beef up its black ranks.

In its effort to show that it was not discriminating, the Bureau resorted to a device that can only be characterized as sleazy. Closely attached to the FBI in my day and paid for out of a confidential fund were a number of regular informants, most of them working within the Communist Party. Most of these stool pigeons were blacks and for several years practically all of them were reported as employees of the Bureau, which they were not. It was not until the early 1960s, long after my departure from the FBI, that it could point to a substantial number of legitimate black employees.

***

I have made it clear, I believe, that it was J. Edgar Hoover's intention that all of his employees march to the same drummer -- namely himself. You did things his way or out you went. For minor errors or mistakes of judgment, agents were abruptly transferred to far-off places at great hardship to themselves and their families. Hoover's attitude, obviously, was that if you didn't like it here you would quit. But quitting could be disastrous, especially if you were wholly dependent on your salary as most of us were. If you resigned under the slightest fire, you frequently found yourself dismissed with prejudice, which meant that you could never work for the government again. However you were sacked, you could not obtain a recommendation for use in applying for another position. Inquiries as to your background and competence brought nothing from the FBI but remarks so vague and cryptic as to leave the impression that you must have been a spy or worse.

These criticisms are advanced reluctantly, for Hoover made an important contribution to the quality of life in America. The twentieth century has been marked by dizzying changes in our moral and political values. The government must adapt to changing circumstances. At the same time, however, the government must stand as a bulwark against disorder and a pillar of continuity. For millions of Americans Hoover was that bulwark and pillar.

***

Once the war was over, I began looking for some way out of the overly-controlled, overly-structured world of the upper echelons of the FBI. I was getting bored by the job and irritated at the continued demand for overtime work which was no longer critically needed. The problem was how to get out without getting hurt. Then, in the summer of 1946, the opportunity presented itself. Representative Clarence Cannon, a Democrat from Missouri and chairman of the House Appropriations Committee, asked Mr. Hoover to provide his committee with a staff of experts to assist in establishing the proper amounts of money to be given to the various government agencies. I was chosen, and made the change happy in the knowledge that although I was only on loan, I would find some way of not coming back.

So, I reported to the House of Representatives Appropriations Committee in July, 1946. For the next seven years, in several positions in the House, I remained on the congressional staff. I learned a great deal about how our government works, or doesn't, and developed some strong opinions about Federal programs and the people who enact and administer them.

8

CAPITOL HILL

How did I happen to go work for the Congress? It came about because of a practice at the time of the legislative branch of government's borrowing people from the executive branch without compensation; that is, their salaries were still charged to their executive departments or agencies. This enabled the Congress to avoid press criticism for overspending its budget for salaries and wages while using the services of knowledgeable civil servants. Naturally the lending agency suffered in the process but had no recourse, except to grumble, since it depended on congressional largess for its operating budget. A later legislative reorganization act corrected the practice. Although the White House still borrows personnel from other executive agencies without compensating them, the Congress now has to reimburse the lending agency for anyone it borrows.

When I went to the Hill in 1946 the House Appropriations Committee was borrowing skilled people on a short-term basis to build up a professional staff capable of helping it reach informed decisions on providing money to the various government agencies. Director Hoover sent me to aid the committee for this purpose. Eventually I had to resign from the Bureau when a government reorganization act altered the borrowing practice. I did resign but only after I had an interview with the Director in which he assured me that he would welcome me back in the FBI at any time.

The shift from the Bureau to the Congress was decidedly advantageous to me financially. Not only did I get a higher salary but I even got paid for my unused annual leave at the Bureau because of the transfer to another branch of the government. So I bought my first car.

***

Clarence Cannon, the Missouri Democrat who wrote the bible on House parliamentary procedures -- "Cannon's Precedents" -- was chairman of the important Appropriations Committee and wanted me to investigate some of the budget proposals submitted to the Congress by the President. I enjoyed a good deal of leeway -- and also protection. Before the start of an investigation, Cannon and the ranking minority member of the full committee had to sign off on a request for it, in writing, from the chairman and ranking minority member of a subcommittee. Their four signatures -- two Democrats and two Republicans -- guarded me against pressure from individual members. If a congressman with a particular political axe to grind tried to influence the investigation, I would tell him the rules and say I would be glad to accommodate him, if he made the proper arrangements with the concerned chairmen. That usually ended the attempt.

I quickly learned that a congressional investigator can wield a lot of influence in Washington. Given enough money and authority, he can dig up some embarrassing matters on almost anyone he wants to go after. I didn't set out on such a trail or to crusade against evils inherent in the system. I took my appropriation of $150,000 and went to work for a committee controlled by Democrats until January 1947 and then by Republicans for the next two years.

My first assignment was to investigate the work of the Public Housing Administration. PHA's purpose was to lend money to local governments for slum clearance and construction of housing that would be available to low-income people. Their low rents would help lift them out of poverty and enable them to move out of the subsidized apartments, making room for other poor slum dwellers. That was the theory. The trouble was, once they got in, you couldn't budge them out.

Private real estate interests represented by the National Association of Real Estate Boards apparently instigated the investigation and provided me with a great many of the leads followed up by my staff. Six of my staff investigated sixteen housing projects around the country -- I visited several -- and my report detailed the shocking abuses we found due to local politics. A project manager appointed by the mayor was usually unwilling to force tenants to move when their economic status improved. Almost 30 percent earned too much to qualify for the low-rent apartments, but I don't know of any who were dispossessed. And of course the cheaters liked the system and voted in a block for the current city officials.

The struggle to end racial discrimination was just getting started in 1946, and the housing projects were classified as "white," "colored" or "mixed." PHA officials, appealing to the Congress for funds took pride when they could point to "mixed" projects. Like my sister, the Mother Superior of a school in Phoenix, I believed in the equality of all God's children and was pleased to see the officials' success in achieving several integrated projects.

Not so in Chicago. Although the projects on the South Side, the predominantly black section of the city, were presented to the Congress as "mixed," I found that in each of the very large ones, comprising some 8,000 units as I recall, there was only one white family. It seemed obvious that with the exception of the Mother Cabrini project, which had about 60 percent black tenants, the

Chicago housing was intended almost entirely for blacks.

                              ***

Another investigation took me on a two-week visit to the Public
Health Service's narcotics hospital and farm in the beautiful
Bluegrass countryside outside Lexington, Kentucky. I did my
work at the institution on an undercover basis and I learned a lot
there about drug addiction and its treatment.

There was a constant struggle between medical people and drug-
enforcement officers. Many of the hospital's inmates maintained
that they were victims of lax early supervision of the manufacture
and sale of drugs. Longtime patients claimed they had become
hooked before a tightening-up of the drug laws. Until then they
were allowed to buy off-the-counter concoctions that were laced
with addictive drugs. Most of these patients had given up any
hope of "kicking" their habit and returned to the hospital several
times in an effort to reduce their drug tolerance. They suggested
that they be recognized as incapable of complete rehabilitation and
be legally provided with enough narcotics for their minimum
needs.   They claimed they wouldn't abuse this privilege.
Enforcement officials vigorously opposed this "solution," saying
that addicts would cut their drugs and sell what they didn't need
at fantastic prices. Similarly the enforcement people argued that
dope-peddling rings would flourish if a proposed organization of
Narcotics Anonymous ever got off the ground.

I thought this hard-line view was too rigid and that controls could
prevent abuses and remove a very small segment of addicts from
the scourge of a system that had caught them unaware. As a
matter of fact, at the time of my inquiry there was a rather firm
belief among informed people that the drug problem was
decreasing and would soon become a minor one. Experiments
with methadone showed promise of eliminating the terrible stress
of withdrawal. But the war in Vietnam and its effects on soldiers

there and protestors at home blasted those hopes.

Hospital inmates worked the farm as part of their therapy. The farm was supposed to be self-sustaining, but it operated at a substantial loss.   Since tight security was thought to hinder patients' cure, they had little supervision. That lack of oversight may help vouch for a story of how some inmates who had been convicted for using marijuana managed to continue their habit. Marijuana is derived from the hemp plant, which had been a principal crop in the Bluegrass before the Civil War.   Its production revived briefly during World War II, and hemp plants often still grew wild in a field just over an easily climbable fence from the narcotics hospital farm.

Patients who voluntarily committed themselves, some of them famous individuals and a surprisingly large number of doctors, could leave -- or come back -- when they chose to.   They invariably lapsed if they stayed only a few weeks.

My comprehensive report on that interesting investigation resulted in policy changes cutting the number of times a person could return to the hospital for treatment.

***

An investigation of the Bureau of Internal Revenue in 1947 resulted in a flurry of publicity and controversy when my report was released early the next year. In the Boston regional office we found strong evidence that employees wanting promotions were forced to contribute money to the Democratic Party. The head of the office, thought likely to be the party's next gubernatorial candidate, was tried for taking bribes and for falsely certifying that some delinquent taxpayers had discharged liens against them. His conviction was later reversed, but he was dead politically.

We found similar instances of corruption and the use of the tax-collecting power for partisan purposes in other Internal Revenue offices as well. The St. Louis office was the only one about which I said complimentary things; ironically, even the genial Irishman who headed it was later sentenced to a short prison term for tax-fixing.

In the House debate on my report Congressman Gordon Canfield (R, New Jersey) complimented me for the exposure of a "sordid picture" of "waste, inefficiency, corruption and criminality." As he said and as Washington newspapers printed, I received phone calls "threatening to blow [my] brains out" for producing a "very thorough, impartial study." President Truman and his supporters, of course, saw it differently.

One prominent Democrat did get some campaign ammunition from an investigation I conducted of the activities of the U.S. Employment Office in Memphis, Tennessee. My report showing that a number of employees were forced to pay a 10 percent tribute to Boss Ed Crump's political machine helped Estes Kefauver in his campaign for the Senate against the Crump candidate.

***

I made some lifelong friends during my years on the Hill. My first boss, Mr. Cannon, whose skill and acumen I admired, wasn't one of them. His temper and partisanship would later cost me my job. He lost his as chairman of the Appropriations Committee when the fall elections of 1946 overturned the Democratic majorities in the Congress. His successor was John Taber of Auburn, New York.

Taber's tight grasp on the Federal purse strings suited my conservative fiscal views. He raised hell at nearly all spending proposals, and his dislike of any taint of "socialism" checkmated liberals seeking funds for social programs. Actually, I think his method aimed at, and usually achieved, a compromise that saved a lot of money without real damage to worthwhile ends. During his forty years in the House, most of them in the minority, many "temporary" expedients became costly permanent programs, and the national debt rose from a comfortable $25 billion to about $300 billion. It was a frustrating experience for him. "Where will it end?" he would ask.

Taber believed, as I did, that the first step on the path to socialism was the Social Security system, substituting government for personal responsibility and thrift. It's political suicide to try to abolish it. There is -- or was until lately -- a popular misconception that receipts from the payroll tax are earmarked and invested like an annuity to be returned as a pension when one retires. Instead, the money is spent as fast as it comes in to meet current costs of government. As the number of elderly grow, and more people use Social Security, taxes must rise to meet continuously rising costs of the system.

Taber also foresaw one of the consequences of the Marshall Plan designed to rebuild shattered European economies after the end of the second World War. We contributed our treasure, our stockpiles, and our citizens' savings for an initially $13-17 billion dollar program that grew into hundreds of billions. By raising up competitors, some with cheap labor, our foreign trade balances changed from black ink to red and we whittled away our economic supremacy. I never thought the United States would end up in a shooting war with the Soviet Union, but I feared that profligate spending would result in the creation of a socialist state here.

With several notable exceptions, members of Congress treated me kindly and fairly. As a member of the staff I enjoyed the "Privilege of the floor" and could enter the House chamber and stand at the back. One of the most thrilling moments of my life came when I heard General Douglas MacArthur speak to a joint session of the Congress and give his "Old soldiers never die" speech after being fired from his command in Korea by Harry Truman. I wish MacArthur could have been elected President.

***

I also had some amusing experiences on the Hill. I remember one occasion at a Defense Department hearing when Taber asked me to sit between a couple of congressmen who disliked each other. I was supposed to keep the peace between the studious Albert Engel of Michigan, who tolerated no frivolous nonsense, and a man I'll call Charley, who could get nasty when he was oiled up, which was most of the day. Charley was invariably drunk by ten in the morning when the hearings convened. I always hoped he wouldn't show up, but when he did he insulted witnesses, even the Secretary of Defense, and disrupted the proceedings. When his craving for another drink pulled him out of the room we hurried to finish our work before he came back.

Charley's wife gave him a hard time at home, so he came to his office early and started drinking heavily. In mid-afternoon he would sleep off his drunk enough to arrive home reasonably sober. She caught on and would come to his office and try to find his booze; he countered by hiding bottles all over the Capitol. Norris Cotton, a New Hampshire Representative and later Senator, let Charley stash one of his bottles behind some books in his next-door office. One day Cotton was talking to a Catholic priest when Charley burst through the door, knocked books off the shelf, took a swig, and stomped out. Cotton and the priest pretended to each other that they hadn't even seen Charley's rude caper.

Cotton, a great raconteur, liked to tell me stories of New Hampshire politics, especially those in which Senator Charles Tobey was the butt. During one Republican primary campaign Tobey ranted against a house of prostitution in Concord. Cotton considered Tobey a psalm-singing hypocrite and worked against him in the primary. Tobey, trying to mend his fences after his election, asked the young Cotton where he should be sworn into office. Cotton suggested the steps of the Concord whorehouse.

***

When the Democrats regained control of the House in the Eightieth Congress, Cannon replaced Taber as chairman. Although I had conducted my investigations in a nonpartisan way, I had become a controversial character and Cannon had me pegged as a tool of the Republicans. When I offered my services and those of my staff to Cannon, he said they were no longer needed. He wanted it to appear that I was leaving voluntarily and offered to keep me on for a year if I then returned to the FBI. We jockeyed around for a few weeks, but one morning when I went to the office I couldn't get in. He had ordered the locks changed and taken me and my whole staff off the payroll even though they had been assured of legal protection against removal because of a change of political control in the House.

My friends took the fight to the House floor but of course they lost. The Republicans then hired me as Minority Counsel, with no loss of pay but no secretarial help; at least that forced me to learn to type, a skill that has stood me in good stead.

***

The two years as Chief Investigator under Taber's chairmanship of the Appropriations Committee had led me to discover that I was a Republican. My parents were loyal Democrats, and the only vote I had ever cast -- one I became ashamed of -- was for Franklin D. Roosevelt. But working for the Congress I saw that conservative Republicans' thinking, especially on fiscal matters, agreed with mine. My older brother Ed may have influenced me too since he shared my conservative views on government spending.

Another Republican congressman I admired was a Boston blueblood, Richard B. Wigglesworth. In his undergraduate days at Harvard "Wiggy" was a great quarterback. A "football knee" bothered him the rest of his life and caused him to fall down every once in a while. I suppose Wigglesworth Hall in Harvard Yard is named for one of his ancestors -- not the Puritan preacher whose poem "The Day of Doom" scared the daylights of Bay Colony sinners, but his grandson who was a professor of divinity and acting president of Harvard in the late 1700s. Dick, who became our ambassador to Canada in the Eisenhower Administration, certainly deserves to be remembered as a devoted public servant. All too often people who hold Congress in low esteem lump its finest members along with the unworthy.

***

But some members of Congress are unworthy. Those who pursue their own special interests almost exclusively and are influenced by the money pushing those interests seem to cause scandals nearly every session. I have served in executive and regulatory offices of the Federal government as well as the legislative branch, and I have always resented the double standard that makes it acceptable for a congressman to engage in activities that would put an executive branch "bureaucrat downtown" in the pokey. Members who are lawyers see business gravitating to their firms. Those whose private business interests are regulated by the Federal government -- and which ones aren't? -- are casually wined and dined in ways that may subtly influence their votes.

Other Federal employees can't legally acquire the kind of money from their jobs that members of Congress pick up as political campaign contributions. Campaigns cost a lot of money of course in close districts, but members from "safe" districts often spend only a few hundred dollars while receiving many thousands from contributors who expect special favors in return. They don't have to return the unspent funds. And those from safe districts generally have the most influence over legislation since their seniority has moved them into committee chairmanships. I saw many of them living in luxury while I had to get by on my government salary.

Besides piling up unspent campaign contributions, some members even got kickbacks from members of their staffs. There were several instances of kickbacks in the Eightieth Congress. Congressional rules then permitted a congressman to use his salary allowance as he saw fit. The practice of reducing employees' salaries by kickbacks was far from casual until the government cracked down and sent some distinguished legislators to prison. The few cases I was aware of came to light when a disgruntled employee blew the whistle on his -- or more often her-boss. A congressman deciding to end a romantic affair with a secretary risked exposure by the angry woman scorned.

One member convicted of taking kickbacks was J. Parnell Thomas, a New Jersey Republican who headed the House UnAmerican Activities Committee (HUAC), long a target of liberals all over the country. I had never had any contact with him, but before his trial he phoned me and said he thought I had some information that would help his defense. He arranged to meet me in the lobby of the Statler Hotel in downtown Washington. I took the precaution of asking two members of my staff to observe our meeting surreptitiously. At the meeting Thomas said he had heard that the FBI had a list of sixty-five congressmen who had taken kickbacks and that I knew of the list. I told him I knew of no such list; besides, if I had possessed information of any violation of law, I would have reported it to the proper authorities. I also pointed out the obvious impropriety of my working for the Congress and making any inquiry at all concerning the private affairs of any member. I promptly wrote a memorandum recording the incident, mailed it to myself registered mail, and retained the unopened envelope for years in case questions might arise.

***

I also met Richard M. Nixon on the Hill when he was a freshman member of Congress and a member of the House UnAmerican Activities Committee. I helped him prepare some of his early speeches on the Communist issue, and he consulted me at length on HUAC's investigation of Alger Hiss, a smooth, sophisticated State Department official so highly regarded by liberal internationalists that they easily imagined him as a future Secretary of State, perhaps even President.

One must remember the climate of opinion pervading Washington, and much of the country, just after the war, to understand the furor over the HUAC investigation of espionage so doggedly pressed by Nixon,. The Soviet Union had been our ally and had suffered enormous losses fighting Hitler's armies. I'm sure President Roosevelt thought he could handle Joe Stalin and that the U.S. faced no serious threat from the USSR. A lot of us, though, thought he was making a dreadful mistake in minimizing the Communist menace.

Before I left the FBI we believed Hiss was an agent of a Communist conspiracy dedicated to overthrowing our government. I know J. Edgar Hoover went over the head of the Attorney General and told the President that Hiss was probably a Communist Party agent. Not only did FDR fail to heed this warning, he gave Hiss a sensitive assignment as a policy adviser in our delegation at the San Francisco Conference, held in April and May 1945, just after Roosevelt's death, which drafted the United Nations Charter. He presided in the chair when the conference opened. Ironically, he issued security clearances to participants in the conference, including FBI agents who knew damn well he was a spy. Hiss's eventual conviction of lying to a Federal grand jury gave credibility to Republicans' charges that Democrats were "soft on Communism."

On occasion this anti-Communist zeal could backfire. I recall one case when a lobbyist seeking to gain influence with an important Senator tried to mastermind a scheme to discredit Truman's Secretary of the Interior, Oscar Chapman. The lobbyist acquired a photostat of the oath of office administered to Chapman at his swearing-in. Since it did not contain the usual non-Communist affidavit, the lobbyist jumped to the conclusion that Chapman was a Communist. He worked on the Senator's administrative assistant who sold his boss on making a Senate speech on the matter. Someone a little more cautious asked for my advice. I agreed that the omission of the affidavit looked bad for Chapman, but suspecting that a Cabinet officer would hardly refuse to swear he was not a member of the Communist Party, I suggested it would be wise to ask the Interior Department for an explanation. In fact, I offered to ask the Secretary myself. The Senator's staff thought that would forewarn Chapman and spoil their headline-winning surprise. I shrugged my shoulders and let them go their merry way.

The Senator made his speech on the Senate floor and a hearing on the charges followed promptly. A simple explanation demolished the flimsy accusation. As in other public swearing-in ceremonies, extraneous matters, including the non-Communist portion, were routinely omitted from the oral oath. The Secretary had already properly executed the disclaimer affidavit. The poor Republican Senator, a fine man, had been victimized by the lobbyist and his staff. Sitting through the hearing he heard himself pilloried as a mudslinger and an example of "little men" in high places. I spent several weeks in the Senator's office trying to build a defense for his embarrassing action. While I consulted with other Senators to get the right questions asked when the affair came up on the Senate floor, the impetuous lobbyist took to his bed and stayed drunk and incommunicado. The storm did blow over in time, though it always whipped up again in the Senator's later campaigns.

***

That lobbyist acted foolishly and dangerously. Still, I suppose I'm one of the few people who would say a good word for most lobbyists. The wheelers and dealers', who number quite a few, and the small number of outright crooks should not tar the rank and file. My observation of the congressional process taught me that legitimate lobbyists play an important part in drafting appropriate legislation. They generally know more about their subjects than a member of Congress or his staff. Lobbyists have to contend with competing interests. The careful legislator who double-checks the various views and picks those that fit his agenda can benefit from lobbyists' appeals for their causes.

***

My best friend on the Hill was Senator Styles Bridges of New Hampshire. He liked me and thought I had a talent for getting people out of trouble. As the ranking Republican on the Senate Appropriations Committee he knew of my work on the House side and liked what he saw. He used to ask for my help not only for himself but for other Republican Senators -- the one making the reckless charges against Oscar Chapman, for example -- who needed some research done. His sponsorship was mainly responsible for my later appointment to the FCC.

Late in 1950 Senator Bridges recommended me to Robert A. Taft of Ohio for the important position of Chief of Staff of the Republican Policy Committee. Unfortunately, too many of my friends on their own initiative started a campaign on my behalf which Taft viewed as pressure and resented. He and Bridges had quite a row and Taft refused to yield. I was disappointed but I rather admired Taft's stand. I learned a valuable lesson: Sometimes your friends are your worst enemies.

Taft didn't court popularity but took principled stands on issues.

I would say a good word for most members of Congress as I came to see them at work during my seven years on the Hill. They live, of course, in a goldfish bowl and are constantly being pressured by someone at home for some kind of special favor. Most of them work hard and are devoted to the national interest as they see it as well as the interests of their constituents. I was frequently annoyed by the comments of visitors who came to the House and Senate galleries and, seeing so few members on the floor engaging in debate, concluded that those absent were idlers neglecting their public responsibility. Those visitors didn't realize that the real work of Congress goes on in committee rooms and in the dungeons of the Capitol, often far into the night. I was annoyed, too, by stories in the press by reporters and columnists eager to clobber members they disliked. Leaks to the press from a partisan opponent or his staff sometimes get congressmen in trouble. I suffered myself from a leak by a member of my staff, a secretary whose boyfriend was under surveillance by agents of another government agency. They told me in confidence that she was telling him of my Internal Revenue Bureau investigation. He had worked for the bureau and passed the information to friends there. I couldn't confront her without destroying the surveillance, but I did contrive to plant some false information, which must have caused consternation at the bureau. And when I verified the facts in an anonymous letter detailing the time, the hotel, and false registration of a trip she and her boyfriend made to New York, she promptly complied with my request for her resignation. To her credit, she turned down his suggestion of retaliating against me by accusing me of making passes at her.

As is often said, Congress is a sieve -- as are the White House and executive departments and agencies. In popularity polls politicians vie with newspapermen for bottom ranking. One of the many criticisms leveled at Congress is the system of seniority for choosing committee chairmanships. Still, I think it's the only way in which the practical work of the Congress can be carried out. It does bring some weak members to the top, but it results in stability in the legislative process.

The end result of the legislative process -- that is, the enactment
of laws passed by both houses of the Congress and approved by
the President -- generally impressed me favorably, even though
the wire-pulling and efforts to push selfish parochial claims irked
me.   The framers of the Constitution evidently expected that
members of the House of Representatives, elected directly by the
people, would advocate and guard the special concerns of their
local districts. Senators, on the other hand, were to be chosen by
state legislatures and presumably would take the broader interests
of their states and indeed the whole country into account. Their
choice by state legislatures aroused a storm of popular criticism
early in the twentieth century when reformers revealed scandalous
purchases by rich men or big trusts or corporations of enough
votes in state houses to win seats in the U.S. Senate. The result
was the adoption of the Seventeenth Amendment to the
Constitution providing that Senators too should be chosen by
direct vote of the people.

While this change no doubt made our national legislature appear
to be more "democratic," I have always been concerned about one
aspect of direct election of Senators. It seems to me that it has
destroyed the balance between the two houses.   In effect, the
Senator is just another congressman and must take the narrow
view of the selfish interest of his state if he expects to return after
the next election.

                              ***

I treasure the memory of my seven years on the Hill, though one
investigation resulted in some unwanted -- and undeserved --
notoriety that I'll relate in the next chapter. I believe my efforts,
and that of my hard-working staff, made some valuable
contributions to the country. At least, a special issue of a popular
magazine of the time -- Flair -- named me in November 1950 as

one of the ten wise young men of Washington. I was in good company, along with Frank Pace, Jr., Eugene M. Zukert, Paul H. Nitze, and other future luminaries. It also credited me with saving the taxpayers five billion dollars during the past two years.

Bob Lee, dancing with his wife, Wilma "Rex" Rector Lee, 1961.

9

JOE McCARTHY

Joe McCarthy was my friend. I am proud of that fact, and, yet, it has haunted me for years. I cringe when I hear his name with "ism" tacked on, bandied about carelessly in political debate, or see it defined in the dictionary as "[t]he use of methods of investigation and accusation regarded as unfair, in order to suppress opposition." For it was my investigation and his misuse of it that launched his meteoric Senate career and his tragic fall five years later. I treasure the memory of his friendship and that of his lovely wife, despite the heartaches it caused for me and my family.

To me, Senator Joseph R. McCarthy of Wisconsin was a good man who went wrong. He had one of the sharpest minds I ever met and an imagination that, unfortunately, was too little troubled by facts. In Senate hearings or floor debate, as in the boxing ring in college, he was a brawler whose wild swings quickly turned him from cornered defendant to relentless attacker. He played the game of politics with reckless abandon and a ruthless determination to win, whatever the cost. Still, he possessed a kind of boyish innocence, an engaging grin, and a playful fondness of pranks. He sometimes seemed oblivious of the hurt he inflicted. After savaging the Department of State, he encountered its head in a Senate elevator. "Hello, Dean," Joe said, and was baffled by

117

Acheson's angry glare.

Joe McCarthy was in a very real sense a product of his times --
times that in retrospect are difficult to understand.   Wartime
distrust of our ally, the Soviet Union, soon turned to fear, which
grew as the communists consolidated their hold on eastern Europe
and threatened to overturn western democratic governments. Cold
War anxieties intensified with the Berlin blockade and airlift, the
successes of communist armies in China, and the withdrawal of
American troops from Korea.   In 1949-50 we learned that the
Russians could already produce atomic explosions and had
perhaps learned the "secret" of the A-bomb from traitors -- like
the British physicist Klaus Fuchs, who confessed to spying for the
USSR while working at Los Alamos. On January 21, 1950, two
weeks before Fuchs's arrest in London, Alger Hiss was convicted
of perjury. And six days after Fuchs's arrest Joe McCarthy made
a famous speech in Wheeling, West Virginia, about Communists
in the State Department.

***

To explain my involvement in McCarthy's sensational charges, I
have to go back to 1947. Sometime early that year, the House
Appropriations Committee asked me to investigate the efficiency
of the State Department and submit my report at the next
congressional session. The directive, which gave me a good deal
of latitude, was signed, as usual, by the chairmen and ranking
minority members of the subcommittee and the full committee.

I immediately set up a task force for a big job -- to study every
organizational unit in the department. I had recently hired two ex-
FBI men whom I had known and admired for a good many years
-- Eugene Rinta, a skilled accountant and former All-American
basketball player at Ohio University, and Harris Huston, who had
worked with me at FBI headquarters; Huston later served with
distinction as American Consul General in Curacao. Both men

shared my concern about the danger of Communist subversion. They examined in detail 108 personnel folders of State Department employees and prospective employees and were shocked by the lax practices they found in the Department's handling of security matters.

I must emphasize that the 108 individuals were not all suspected security risks. Quite a few of them had absolutely no derogatory information in their files; indeed, we wondered why the Department failed to hire some of this group while choosing others whose files revealed questionable associations. There were no identified Communists in the list, but some persons allegedly connected with subversive organizations were hired without running down the facts.

The list of 108 individuals was appended to our comprehensive report on the operations of the State Department, and we merely suggested that questions it raised might be explored in subsequent hearings. Individuals were identified simply by number, and only the committee chairmen received the key linking numbers to names. The report was confidential and distributed to members of the Appropriations Committee and the House UnAmerican Activities Committee. But nothing in Congress stays confidential very long, as recent-investigations and hearings have demonstrated, and I assumed the report would one day reach the light of day.

My summary of the report emphasized the inefficiency, waste, and overstaffing with high-salaried officials throughout the various operating areas of the department. Closely related political, economic, cultural, and intelligence matters were separated organizationally and physically. They needed to be consolidated vertically to eliminate an endless series of conferences; the slow movement of staff papers up and down through various units; petty reviews of the content of papers and letters and picayune changes requiring retyping -- e.g., from "receipt is acknowledged" to "the receipt is acknowledged." We concluded that reorganization of the Department's vast horizontal structure offered a possibility of "a tremendous savings in personnel and energy."

My summary also said that the Department's investigative division should have more management authority and less control from above. I found that employees of questionable loyalty remained on the rolls for many months, often a year or more, while they are being investigated and re-investigated, simply because no one in the long chain of case evaluators would take definite action. Other employees of questionable loyalty remained un-investigated.

Little did I realize then the twist of fate that would plop this report into the eager hands of Joe McCarthy. But he was looking for a springboard into the national spotlight, and, unintentionally, I'd given it to him.

This document, summarizing my findings, became known as the "Lee Report." The press gave the report some modest coverage when the House hearings were made public some months later. People who read it concluded that the State Department's personnel-security procedures were decidedly careless, but no one discerned a sinister subversive plot.

I forgot all about the report until February 1950. Then press reports of Joe McCarthy's Wheeling speech and others he gave while plane-hopping around the country the next few days startled me into awareness that the list of 108 people in the report's appendix provided the basis of his charges. Just how many "card-carrying Communists" McCarthy alleged to be in the State Department soon turned into a confusing "numbers game," since at various times he gave quite different figures -- 205, "more than 200," 57, 81, and maybe others.

The Senator inserted my report in the <u>Congressional Record</u>. But he had made important alterations of my report's data and profiles. The numbers we had assigned to individuals had been changed, and the tampering with excerpts included additional information and a generous sprinkling of loaded adjectives. He could have presented a much stronger case, I have always believed, if he had stuck to the factual summaries we had written. They weren't colorful enough, though, for him.

***

I did not give the list to McCarthy as some writers have said. Indeed, I had never even met the Senator before his sensational Lincoln Day speeches. He always claimed that "loyal" State Department employees had provided his data from their examination of personnel files. And despite my later friendship with Joe, which nearly ruined my career, he never admitted to me that my report was his source. Other people, however, thought I had fed Joe his information, and I have often wondered why I was not called as a witness in the Senate investigation triggered by his charges. I think it may have been because an unwritten congressional policy barred calling a staff member of the "other body" from giving testimony. Too bad, because I could have set the record straight and perhaps helped Joe avoid his later trauma.

***

My good friend Senator Styles Bridges, for whom I had done some trouble shooting, thought I could help keep Joe from blundering onto dangerous ground. He phoned me one afternoon and asked me to come to his apartment in the Dorchester House that evening. Other Republicans present were Senators Richard Nixon and William Knowland of California and Karl Mundt of South Dakota, Representative John Taber of New York, and Bridges' administrative assistant, Scott McLeod -- and Joe, whom I met for the first time.

Joe made a powerful impression on me. He was physically rugged and had the most penetrating eyes I had ever seen. But though he had a sharp mind, he was abysmally ignorant of communism in general and of the Communist Party's tactics in particular. When the name of the party's general secretary in the United States came up, Joe turned to me and asked, "Who is Earl Browder?" Obviously he was in way over his head.

That meeting began an entanglement between Joe and myself that lasted for the next three years. And not just the two of us. His then secretary, Jean Kerr, in digging up information for his speeches kept in constant touch with me. My wife and I spent many evenings at Jean's house in Northeast Washington talking over strategy for his crusade. Rex and Jean became the closest of friends. In fact, Rex was Jean's matron of honor when she and Joe were married at St. Matthew's Cathedral in one of Washington's largest weddings ever; nearly every notable Republican except President Eisenhower was there and the Pope sent his blessing to the couple.

When Joe went to Wheeling to begin his Lincoln Day hops around the country for the Republican Party he carried drafts of two speeches -- one on Communists in the government and the other on Federal housing policy. One of the men driving him to town from the airport told him the speech would be broadcast over a local radio station; he thought the speech about Communists would have the greater appeal and Joe readily agreed. How different it would have been if he had talked about housing instead! And if the Lincoln Day speeches hadn't come on a dull - news weekend, reporters wouldn't have given his claims such great play. Most of what he had to say, after all, was a pretty standard partisan attack on Democrats for being soft on Communism.

But the enormous publicity given Joe's charges captured the attention of people all over the country. Already worried about

Soviet nuclear weapons, the collapse of resistance to communist armies in Asia, and the betrayal of our secrets and plans by scientists like Fuchs and high officials like Hiss, many American citizens reacted with dismay and fear. They were ready to believe Joe's exaggerations about Communists in the State Department, no matter how confused they were by his daily shifting numbers. And Joe, who I think had started this public excitement as a lark, soon began to believe his wild story himself.

Republicans seized on the public alarm as a way to regain control of Congress and the presidency. Democrats naturally tried not only to discredit Joe but to convince voters that they, too, were security-conscious anti-Communists, but sensibly so. In the Senate they counterattacked in a hearing chaired by Millard Tydings, a conservative Maryland Democrat who said he wanted "neither a witch hunt . . . nor a whitewash." But the Democratic majority report following the hearing called McCarthy's charges "[a] fraud and a hoax perpetrated on the Senate of the United States and the American people." The report infuriated Joe's partisans who vowed to oust Tydings from his Senate seat. Nor did the report quiet the anxieties of the American public. The very day it was released the FBI announced the arrest of Julius Rosenberg for wartime espionage. Tydings' report, Republican newspapers and conservative radio commentators told their audiences, was indeed a "whitewash" of years of Democrats' indifference to the danger posed by Communist spies and subversives.

The liberal and left-wing press, on the other hand, vilified Joe. He certainly deserved some of the abuse heaped on him, but I thought it was overdone. Under the mantle of free speech and congressional immunity from prosecution, other Senators, before and since, have gotten away with similar outrageous behavior. Nor did the aloof, aristocratic Millard Tydings win the adoration of plain American citizens who feared that there was a real danger to their country no matter how much McCarthy exaggerated it.

***

The Republican Party made good use of the fanatical, often unquestioning support McCarthy enjoyed among many voters. In the fall elections of 1950 he helped elect to the Senate Herman Welker of Idaho and John Marshall Butler of Maryland (who defeated Tydings). Two years later, when Eisenhower won the presidency, Joe played an important part in defeating another bitter enemy, Senator William Benton of Connecticut, and replacing him with Prescott Bush (the ex-President's father) and in electing Barry Goldwater of Arizona. I participated on the periphery of some of these races.

My help -- and my wife's -- in defeating Tydings was more than peripheral. FDR hadn't been able to "purge" the conservative Maryland senator in 1938, but the storm over Tydings' effort to destroy McCarthy contributed greatly to his defeat for reelection a dozen years later.

I accompanied Joe on a trip to Chicago in 1950, the year Everett M. Dirksen won his first campaign for the Senate, and then in GOP bigwig Walter S. Hallanan's private plane back to Wheeling, West Virginia. In Wheeling, Joe spent a lot of time on the phone talking to Jon M. Jonkel, a Chicago advertising man who was managing the campaign of Tydings' Republican opponent, John Marshall Butler. Joe didn't trust Jonkel and thought he was dipping into the till of Butler's campaign funds and diverting money intended for a pet postcard project Joe had in mind. Joe's idea was simple. The back of a hand-addressed card bearing a picture of Butler would carry the message: "I shall be deeply grateful for your vote next Tuesday." The cards were to be mailed on the weekend just before the election. I suppose a lot of people thought John Butler had signed the cards himself -- a mild subterfuge but one not criticized in subsequent congressional investigations, and in fact praised as a sensible way to contact voters.

I told Joe I thought Rex would take on the postcard project as she was eager to help him get revenge against Tydings. She readily agreed when we phoned her, and I took the next plane home to get the project started.

The next day in Joe's office I met Alvin M. Bentley, a Michigan industrialist who later became a member of Congress; he was one of those seriously injured when Puerto Rican nationalists shot up the House of Representatives chamber. He gave me a $5,000 check made out to the Butler campaign to be used for the postcard project, and I was to take it to Baltimore and have Jonkel endorse it over to Rex. Jonkel endorsed it reluctantly; he apparently had little faith in the project and thought the money could be used more effectively elsewhere. While I was in his office he asked me to do him a favor on a delicate political matter. He said he didn't fully trust his own campaign organization and wanted me to deliver a package, which I guessed contained a lot of money. At the Baltimore address he gave me, an insurance office, I handed the package to Jake Pollack, who called Jonkel in my presence and acknowledged receiving the funds. I later heard that Pollack, who controlled a large block of Baltimore votes, delivered them to Butler in a deal double-crossing Tydings and contributing to his defeat. Later investigations showed that Jonkel failed to report a good many contributions, including the check I handed him. I was called before the grand jury which indicted him and he was subsequently found guilty and paid a $5,000 fine.

The postcard campaign disrupted my home the next few weeks. We enlisted hundreds of women to write voters' addresses and Butler's message, and some fifty thousand cards were mailed from various places in Maryland. I'm sure they contributed to Tydings' defeat.

Another campaign photograph used against Tydings was really dirty politics. Neither Rex nor I had anything to do with putting together the famous "cropped" picture, a "composite" of two

photos which were slickly arranged to show Tydings appearing to
be talking to the communist party chief, Earl Browder. (By now
Joe knew who Browder was.) I have never doubted that Joe at
least sanctioned the deceptive act.

***

Joe's effort to defeat Tydings may not have been the determining
factor in the election -- some students of politics think it was
overrated -- but it gave him tremendous clout. Even his bitter
enemies seemed to consider him the most powerful man in
America. Republicans seeking office, even moderates, asked for
his help. I remember witnessing an interesting exchange between
Joe and Henry Cabot Lodge of Massachusetts, who was
campaigning for the Senate in 1952 against John F. Kennedy.

Lodge had been one of the two Republican Senators in the
Tydings hearing and had written a minority report calling the
investigation "superficial and inconclusive." Maybe Lodge's
defense wasn't strong enough to suit Joe. At any rate, he disliked
Lodge and friendship for the Kennedy family triumphed over
party loyalty. Joe was a frequent guest of Joseph Kennedy at
Hyannisport, and I believe the conservative patriarch was helping
finance his anti-communist crusade. Joe sometimes dated Eunice
and Patricia Kennedy; when Eunice married Sargent Shriver, Joe
sent a "loser's" congratulations.

Joe hoped Jack Kennedy would unseat Lodge. As Joe was
extremely popular in Massachusetts, Lodge sought his help. Joe
and I were in his room in the Blackstone Hotel in Chicago when
Lodge called and asked Joe to campaign for him. That put Joe on
the spot but he got out of it. He said, "Cabot, I will be glad to
come out and speak for you, and I want you to arrange it and
introduce me from the platform." Joe knew Lodge would find that
impossible. Lodge, wanting to keep in good odor with anti--
McCarthy voters, said he couldn't do that and suggested that Joe

arrange for some American Legion group to invite him. Joe said simply, "Screw you!" I have often wondered what the course of history might have been if Lodge had won that election and the young Jack Kennedy's road to the White House had dead-ended.

One of Joe's financial backers was the Texas billionaire H.L Hunt. My occasional association with Hunt began in 1953. For several years he had sponsored a print and radio program called "Facts Forum," which aimed to inform people about the menace of communism and what he foresaw as the degradation of economic and political liberty. He came to see me to tell me of his interest in starting a television program along the same line and thought I might be interested in moderating some of the discussions. I examined the project very carefully and considered it worthwhile. I still think it was. Despite the program's conservative orientation it did present the other side of issues. The FCC received very few complaints about it.

I told Mr. Hunt I thought he had a good idea. I told him I didn't want any money for undertaking the job and he didn't offer me any. I then asked Jean Kerr for her assistance.

I did two or three shows for Mr. Hunt and they were terrible. The first was a debate between Joe McCarthy and Democratic Senator Warren Magnuson of Washington. During the pre-telecast warmup, Joe outlined his position on the conflict in Korea and Magnuson indicated he did not disagree basically. I told them I wanted a lively debate, not a love feast. Magnuson chuckled and suggested that Joe call Secretary of State Dean Acheson some nasty names and then he would become angry. That tactic worked; they went at each other hammer and tongs, pounding on the table and screaming at one another. If any viewers of the program saw our congenial dinner together later, they must have thought that politicians are awful hypocrites.

Another show was a lot worse. This time I paired Senator Allen

Ellender (D, Louisiana) and Congressman John Phillips (R, California). One good thing: the program taught me something about television technique. The audio part was all right but not the picture. The film was shot in color and no make-up was used. Television is hardly a flattering visual medium at best, and a fairly heavy beard gives a man a dour look. I blamed Mr. Hunt for not spending his money for professional help and Jean and I sent his $200 expense money back and told him he needed it more than we did. He never acknowledged the letter. Some years later I was asked in a congressional hearing if I had ever received any money from H.L. Hunt. I got a big laugh when I told about the $200 and was informed that I needed a guardian if I was going to send money to the richest man in the world.

I had many contacts with Mr. Hunt over the years. They began when he backed Joe in the early 1950s and continued long after. Leaving Joe for the moment, I'll jump ahead to relate a little of my later association with H.L. Hunt.

During my years on the FCC I made hundreds of appearances before industry and public groups, and God only knows on how many TV spots and programs. One of the most interesting was in Dallas, in 1961. An old friend from FBI days asked me to appear before the Radio and Television Executives of Texas and I accepted the invitation. Mr. Hunt saw the news stories announcing my visit and asked me if I would address a group he would organize on the subject of "Patriotism 1961." I told him I didn't want to get into any controversy about internal security but agreed to make the speech. Later I was rather ashamed at my hesitance to stand up and speak out forthrightly about my convictions. But he was a controversial character, and I had been, and the beatings I had taken before from the liberal press made me chary. He was rich and could disdain his critics, but I had to make a living and I didn't want to endanger that.

Since my wife was not going to accompany me on the trip, I

declined Mr. Hunt's invitation to stay at his home. When the plane landed in Texas the stewardess told me there was a crowd of reporters wanting to see me and, by the way, who the hell was I? To my surprise, in addition to the horde of reporters.Mr. Hunt himself was on hand to greet me. He had arranged for a press conference at the airport, which lasted about an hour, and then drove me to my hotel. That night I was amazed to find an audience of about 500 people who had paid to hear me. The cream of Dallas society, they were conservative to the core and sick of Washington interference in their lives. Women questioners pressed me on why the Federal government allowed so much crime and violence on television. I tried to point out to this "Lifeline" group the inconsistency of their views: Always the first to complain about government intervention, they nevertheless thought the FCC should do something to get more conservative commentators like Fulton Lewis, Jr., on the air. I told them my bitterest enemy in Washington was probably Drew Pearson but I would fight hard to ensure his right to express his views. That seemed to impress them.

Driving back from a speech I made the following day at Dallas University, I summoned enough courage to ask Mr. Hunt just how much money he had. He said he had no idea but was sure there was no one alive who could buy him out. A cocktail party that afternoon and another banquet where I spoke again left me exhausted. But before I could collapse in bed H.L. wanted me to meet Pat Boone, the singer who was in Dallas making a movie. We talked about Communism in show business and the clean-cut young man told me of the trouble he had with his network show because he insisted on singing the "Star Spangled Banner" and could not understand why the producers objected.

At H.L.'s insistence I spent the night at his home, a replica of George Washington's Mount Vernon mansion. Sightseeing buses drove by the place as we sat on the porch in the morning; people wanted to get a gander at the house and maybe even spot the richest man in America. I asked H.L. about his reputation as a gambler; Ruth Sheldon Knowles' book The <u>Greatest Gamblers,</u> which he gave me, says he got his start in the oil business by winning an oil lease in a poker game. He said he didn't smoke or drink and had even given up his greatest pleasure -- gambling -- though he was so good professional gamblers refused to play against him.

H.L. Hunt made many enemies. His detractors considered him an extreme reactionary and anti-Semite. I got to know him well on my many trips to Dallas and learned of his kindnesses and good works. When he learned of Rex's serious illness he suggested that she visit, as his guest, a spa which is said to have great healing powers. The spa, an old Indian spring, he had bought, characteristically, sight unseen. I cherish his kindness to Rex and me and his friendship, as I do Joe McCarthy's.

***

There's no need for me to retell the painful story of Joe's decline and fall. When I first met him, in 1950, I believed in his cause and wanted to help it succeed. I was young and ambitious. It made me feel good to associate with powerful men who called me "Bob" and seemed to consider me their equal -- more than their equal in my knowledge of internal-security matters. And in Joe I saw dazzling potential, a man who might with careful handling reach the White House.

But Joe became a zealot, as were some of his advisers. Before long I tried to redirect his energies into other causes. Friends of mine in the investigative unit of the Government Accounting Office told me they would love to have someone with Joe's talents pursue a number of causes involving government fraud. He chaired the same investigative committee that had catapulted Harry Truman to the office of Vice President. My friend Frederick ("Fritz") Coudert, a Republican congressman from the "Silk Stocking District" of New York City, agreed with me that

Joe's hunt for Communists had gone as far as it could profitably go. But Joe, then at what turned out to be the zenith of his influence and popularity, told me he would never give up his battle.

My pleas evidently irritated him and he didn't even speak to me for several months. I heard from other people that he believed Bob Lee had somehow been captured by the Communists who were now using me to end his holy "Fight for America," as he called it in the title of a book he compiled. Ironically, the inscription he penned in a copy to me reads: "To Bob Lee for his contribution to the Fight for America. Wish I could have done as well." That was as much of an acknowledgment as I ever got from him that my 1947 report had launched his astonishing and ultimately tragic crusade.

10

A CONTROVERSIAL APPOINTMENT

After six years on the Hill I began to think about moving on to some other kind of work. If life begins at forty, I was a year beyond that milestone in 1953. With a wife, and three children in Catholic schools, my salary of $11,500 a year as Director of Surveys and Investigations for the House Appropriations Committee was stretched pretty thin.

I had attached my hopes for advancement to Joe McCarthy's bright star. But, Joe had become a single-minded zealot with a mission to fulfill. I had been unable to persuade him to quit his "Fight for America" crusade and take up another cause. My connection with him had received considerable notice in the press, and liberal columnists like Drew Pearson, Doris Fleeson, and Marquis Child had tagged me as Joe's faithful servant. We were still friends, but in some respects his friendship had become a liability. The new Republican President, Dwight Eisenhower, who treated Joe warily, hated his guts.

I had to have a nomination from Eisenhower for a job I hoped to get. The Assistant Comptroller General, Frank Yates, had died recently and many of my friends on the Hill were pushing me as his successor. It would have meant a fifteen-year appointment at a substantially higher salary. John Taber, my last boss in

Congress, was my principal sponsor and as always I had the support of Senator Styles Bridges. I solicited the help of other friends in Congress, from both houses, and delivered to the White House endorsements from about ninety of them. Joe McCarthy wasn't one of them -- I saw to that.

I had an influential friend at the White House in General Wilton B. (Jerry) Persons, one of Eisenhower's principal aides. I spoke to him several times and also to Leonard Hall, chairman of the Republican National Committee. What I didn't know was that Eisenhower had already made a commitment to Lindsay Warren, the former Comptroller General, who was sponsoring Frank Weitzel, a longtime member of the General Accounting Office (GAO) staff. In view of my strong congressional support, the White House had a problem.

While this possible appointment was hanging fire, I set off for Europe in August 1953 on an investigative task for the Appropriations Committee. Often when members of Congress travel abroad, usually on quite legitimate fact-finding endeavors, the press portrays their journeys as frivolous and expensive junkets. Their trips, I knew, would yield better information, more quickly, and at less expense to the taxpayer if competent investigative staff members went to the overseas sites first and had a report ready for the congressmen when they arrived. I proposed to make such a preparatory investigation of a number of matters concerning construction projects in Europe and certain aspects of the U.S. Information Agency. I arranged with the GAO to have some of its staff who were assigned to Europe meet me in London in preparation for the survey.

During my three weeks in London we investigated the purchase by our government of a palatial mansion once owned by the Rothschild family. Winthrop Aldrich, the U.S. ambassador to the Court of St. James's, wanted it refurbished to use as his residence. The contract specified that the mansion be transferred to the buyer in "useable condition." We hardly expected to find works of art once there, but we were surprised to discover an empty shell. Gone were the marble stairs, and plaster of Paris and gilt paint had replaced gold trim. Somehow my report on the ravaged edifice never saw the light of day. I advised against using the building for the ambassador's residence. When Congressman John Phillips arrived in London with other members of the visiting Appropriations Committee, he dashed off a handwritten letter to me saying he agreed; he was indignant about the architect chosen for the restoration job, the huge expense it would require, and the fact that the State Department had decided to go ahead with it apparently without authorization.

Then on to Paris for the next phase of the investigation. There, around the first of October, I received a phone call from my friend Bob Humphreys, director of public relations for the Republican National Committee, suggesting that I get home fast. The White House wanted to see me.

***

In the summer, before I left for Europe, I had been asked if I would be interested in a possible appointment to the FCC. I was doubtful; I didn't know much about the FCC, and its budget and functions were minuscule compared to those of big departments like Defense and Agriculture I might tackle if the GAO appointment came through. But after checking with Taber and Bridges, I had said I would be interested.

It was the FCC appointment that occasioned Bob Humphreys' call. I booked passage on the next flight to New York. Immediately after I arrived I called the White House and someone in charge of appointments scheduled me to meet with Sherman Adams, the former New Hampshire governor who was now the President's chief of staff. I had a long chat with Governor Adams, who said I had checked out favorably for an appointment

to the FCC and he was going to recommend me. He took me in
to see the President and we talked for about thirty minutes, mainly
about educational television. He suggested I contact his brother
Milton, a university president who was interested in the subject.
(I did, but never got a reply to my letter.) They told me to keep
quiet; if my prospective appointment leaked out, it would be
canceled. So I spent the weekend in hiding, scared to death that
backers of some other candidate for the position would find out
a complete unknown in the field of radio and television had been
anointed instead.

For months the trade press had speculated about who would
fill the vacancy on the Commission.   During the summer
theseveral people being considered seemed to have sifted down to
one -- Robert J. Dean.   In fact, reports said that Dean had
arranged to transfer ownership of his radio station in Rapid City,
South Dakota, and that his nomination was on the way to the
Senate when it was suddenly called back for reconsideration.

Luckily that didn't happen to me. They wanted me sworn in right
away, and just three hours after President Eisenhower had signed
my commission, I took the oath of office on October 6, 1953, in
the FCC meeting room. Why the rush I don't know. I learned
later that the appointment and the hurry-up oath-taking came as a
complete surprise to FCC Acting Chairman Rosel Hyde. Quite
properly, he felt miffed that he hadn't been filled in earlier. He
didn't know me from Adam, and I heard he inquired what kind of
Bible was needed since I was said to look Jewish. A photo of the
ceremony in <u>Broadcasting-Telecasting</u> shows me wearing a loud
tie and a broad grin while Chief Judge Harold Stephens of the
U.S. Court of Appeals for the District of Columbia reads the oath
and FCC Commissioner Robert T. Bartley holds the Bible -- both
Testaments -- on which my left hand rests. The photograph
doesn't show the on-looking audience, mostly FCC employees
wondering where this guy came from.

The appointment was controversial from the start. The same issue of Broadcasting-Television pointed out that instead of the "practical broadcaster" the administration had been saying it wanted, it had got "a G-man with a flair for figures." Besides that, he was a friend and political associate of Joe McCarthy. And was it coincidence that McCarthy was backing a Hearst Corporation effort to get a Milwaukee television channel for commercial use, an assignment that would endanger the city's schools' plan to use a channel for educational television? I'm afraid a lot of people doubted my statement to a Washington Post reporter that "I never asked McCarthy to do anything and I'm sure he didn't." Joe and Jean were honeymooning in the Bahamas, and I thought the appointment would be news to him. I also told the reporter that on FCC matters Joe would to get the same treatment as anyone else as far as I'm concerned." And I meant it.

No matter what I said, though, many people were astonished that Eisenhower would award a friend of McCarthy's. Some interpreted the appointment as a move to conciliate the party's right wing. But two scholars suggest that the real reason behind my appointment lay in the earlier organized campaign, led by Representative Taber and Senator Bridges, to get me named Assistant Comptroller General. "What do you do," they ask, "with a person who has 100 congressional endorsements and the support of a determined Styles Bridges?"

The appointment was an interim one. Not until Congress returned to business in January would the nomination go to the Senate. Since my place at the Commission table tipped the balance -- four of the seven members were now Republicans -- many Democratic Senators were sure to swallow hard before voting to confirm a friend of Joe McCarthy. The trio of liberal columnists I mentioned above -- Pearson, Fleeson, and Childs -- harped on my McCarthy ties and revived memories of the dirty tricks used against Tydings in 1950. So too did liberal newspapers like the St. Louis Post-Dispatch. Usually FCC nominees breezed through the confirmation process without even a hearing. This time there would be one.

As a recess appointee I wasn't even on the government payroll. How was I to manage to pay the mortgage, feed and clothe my family, and pay fees to three separate schools without a salary coming in regularly? I had to borrow money and hope that the Senate acted quickly to confirm my appointment to a seven-year term on the Commission, enabling me to draw my $15,000 annual salary and pay back the borrowed money. My possible non-confirmation was a dismal prospect I didn't want to face.

I figured I needed about $2,000 to see me through until the Senate acted on my nomination -- provided I was lucky and the vote came early in the session. So I went to Washington's old City Bank and asked for that amount. They remembered my dealings with them from my FBI days when I had deposited a lot of money in the Bureau's insurance fund built up from agents' contributions when one of their fellows was killed. A tightfisted loan officer finally offered half of what I asked for. That peeved me and I decided to try the Riggs Bank where I got a kinder reception. They offered me $3,000, as I recall, on a ninety-day note. If the Senate acted promptly -- and favorably -- I was all set. If it turned me down, I didn't know what I would have done.

I worried constantly the next three months. The columnists' barbs got under my skin. I learned the hard way how "guilt by association" -- the tactic Joe McCarthy had used so effectively -- could tarnish one's good name. It seemed ironic that his enemies were now turning his smear method on me, his good friend. It was McCarthy they were really seeking to destroy; I was simply a convenient instrument for their vengeance.

I dreaded the ordeal of the confirmation hearing. Still, I wanted it scheduled as soon as possible. As soon as Congress convened in January 1954, I went to see Senator John W. Bricker (R, Ohio), chairman of the Senate Committee on Interstate and Foreign Commerce, and told him my financial predicament and of my desire for an early confirmation. He scheduled my hearing before the committee for January 18. Meanwhile I had been ducking requests for interviews and turning down speech invitations. Senator Robert Kerr (D, Oklahoma) was one of my wise counselors who suggested that I keep my mouth shut and "saw wood." I spent my time learning all I could about the history and functions of the FCC both by reading and on the new job at the Commission. I carefully avoided associating with McCarthy.

The Senate committee grilled me for about three hours, particularly about my qualifications for the job though I knew their real concern was my relationship to McCarthy. I nearly panicked when Joe walked into the hearing room to see what was going on. I was afraid his appearance would ruin my chances. My main adversary on the committee, as he was later during the debate on the Senate floor, was Senator Mike Monroney, an Oklahoma Democrat. After the fight was all over we became good friends. I must have done a fairly good job handling his and other Senators' questions. One Democratic Senator, Edwin C. Johnson of Colorado, wrote saying I had handled myself "extremely well" in answering tough questions in a "straightforward" manner. At any rate the committee recommended me favorably with only one abstention, that of John 0. Pastore (D, Rhode Island). (In my third confirmation hearing, fourteen years later, the friendly Rhode Island Senator told me, "The only thing I have against your appointment is that you are a Republican.")

I sat in the Senate gallery during the debate on the committee's favorable recommendation. The roll call vote -- the first ever for an FCC Commissioner, I believe -- was whiteknuckle time since I had real doubts as to the outcome. It was a great relief when Democrat Earle Clements of Kentucky, the first to vote as the names were called alphabetically, said "Aye!" But there was still a way to go, and I heard enough Senators say "Nay" to scare me. In the end, though, the votes against me tallied only 25 to 58 for. Most of those in the negative, I knew, were really votes against Joe McCarthy. Democratic Senators divided evenly; three Republicans -- George Aiken and Ralph Flanders of Vermont and Margaret Chase Smith of Maine -- voted against me.

The "Nay" votes made me wince, but after the ordeal was over the congratulatory letters I received from members of Congress made me feel proud to have won so many friends during my service on the Hill. Most members of the House Appropriations Committee had written me earlier, after my nomination in October, offering warm congratulations but also what seemed genuine regret that I would no longer be directing investigations for them. Much more than expressing routine good wishes, some congressmen -- I think especially of John Phillips, Fritz Coudert, Mel Laird, Jerry Ford, and Cliff Clevenger -- sounded like they were losing a friend. By this time we were all on a first-name basis. And after the Senate vote a good many Senators wrote too. Several of them were Democrats, particularly southern conservatives. A. Willis Robertson wrote: "Naturally, anyone from Virginia would feel kindly disposed to any man bearing your name. In addition to that, I was fully convinced that there is no member of the Senate who could lead you around by your nose." In that connection, a few congressmen half-jokingly suggested that my presence on the FCC might serve their interests; only one seemed dead serious about it.

**

Not only did my nomination to the FCC teach me the hard way about "guilt by association," I soon learned also about guilt by photo -- this one genuine, unlike McCarthy's "composite" picture of Tydings and Browder. The day after my confirmation a reporter from Time asked me for an interview and came over to my office on Capitol Hill with a photographer. A very pleasant young man, the reporter had evidently not been told that the magazine's editors really wanted a "hatchet job" done on me, or at least if he had, he possessed a higher standard of journalistic ethics than they did. After the next issue of Time appeared I got a call from the young reporter saying he couldn't understand why his story about me hadn't been published. Anyway, he thought I might like to have the pictures the photographer had taken.

There were about sixty candid shots, some very good, some horrible. Several weeks later Life, Time's companion magazine, ran an illustrated piece entitled "McCarthy and His Friends" containing the absolutely worst photo in the batch the reporter had given me. My reaction was about like that of Lyndon Johnson some years later when he saw Peter Hurd's oil portrait of him -- - a rather good one, I thought -- and called it the most "god-awful" thing he had ever seen. The photo of me in Life was a clear case of editorializing by picture if I ever saw one. In fact, I understand that Sol Taishoff, editor and publisher of Broadcasting Magazine, used this as proof that photographers could editorialize to establish their qualification for admission to the press fraternity Alpha Sigma Chi.

About the same time as the Life story, some ex-FBI agents asked me for a picture to run on the front of their magazine. Naturally I picked one of the more flattering ones given to me by the Time reporter. I have kept that cover and the Life story in my scrapbook as an interesting Jekyll-and-Hyde study in contrasts.

***

I went to work at the Commission almost at once after receiving my interim appointment in October. I think I shook hands with every employee there. I got a thorough briefing from the agency's general counsel on what I could and could not do legally. Despite the innuendoes in newspaper stories and columns that I would let Republican partisanship sway my opinions, I was determined to establish my independence and win a reputation for impartiality.

Besides trying to show my Commissioner colleagues and the FCC staff that I was by nature friendly and gregarious, I also read avidly books and articles about the history of communications, especially the development of telegraphy, the telephone, radio, and the fast-growing new field of television. From the "American Leonardo," Samuel F.B. Morse, in the mid-nineteenth century to Ted Turner in the late twentieth, there have been a lot of fascinating, flamboyant, occasionally infuriating personalities associated with the advancement -- and sometimes debasement -- of communications. The accomplishments of inventors and entrepreneurs like Morse, Alexander Graham Bell, Lee de Forest, and David Sarnoff are at least slightly familiar to most educated American citizens. What they know little about is the growth of Federal regulation of communications through the Post Roads Act of 1866, the Interstate Commerce Act of 1887, the Radio Communications Act of 1912, the Radio Act of 1927, and the Communications Act of 1934.

Although I agreed at the time of my joining the FCC -- and still do -- with many of the criticisms of government regulation, the conditions leading to the passage of these acts of Congress clearly showed the need for some central controls over exploding technologies. Through my reading and through my association with professionals in the communications arena, I soon lost my initial uneasiness about plunging into an unfamiliar new activity.

A little about my six fellow Commissioners:

Rosel Hyde, a kindly gentleman of Mormon background and impeccable living habits, had been appointed by President Truman in 1946. He was a Republican but because the Eisenhower Administration had not yet decided on a permanent chairman, he held the office in an acting capacity. He remained as one of my

FCC colleagues until 1969.

John F. Doerfer, a Wisconsin Republican, was a recent Eisenhower appointee. A lawyer with experience handling public utility business, he was named chairman in 1958. He and I became good friends and played a lot of golf together.

Frieda B. Hennock was the only woman member of the Commission -- in fact, the first. She had been a New York lawyer and a close friend of the late Fiorella La Guardia, the colorful mayor of New York City in the 1930s. Despite her left-wing reputation, which was so different from my own, we became good friends. Truman had nominated her for a Federal judgeship, but Pat McCarran (D, Nevada), chairman of the Senate Judiciary Committee, strongly opposed her appointment, as did the New York Bar Association. Senator Robert Taft helped arrange a deal whereby the judgeship nomination was withdrawn and she became a member of the FCC instead.

Edward Webster, the Independent Commissioner, was the only living person who still bore the defunct title of Commodore as a member of the U.S. Coast Guard. A hard worker who took his duties seriously, he did considerable consulting for government and industry after leaving the Commission in 1956.

George Sterling, a Republican from Maine, like career officers in the Foreign Service, had come up through the FCC ranks. He had been an employee of the Commission almost from its start. He left in 1955 under what seemed to me mysterious circumstances. I believe the Eisenhower Administration put pressure on him to resign so that it could appoint George McConnaughery of Ohio as chairman.

Robert T. Bartley, who held the Bible at my swearing-in ceremony, had been on the Commission only a short time. Besides having experience in government, he also knew the business of broadcasting. Shortly after I joined the Commission he took me to see his uncle on Capitol Hill, Sam Rayburn of Texas, the long-time Speaker of the House of Representatives, though temporarily out of that powerful position in the Eighty-Third Congress. I took to heart his advice that it was quite appropriate to use all the influence you could muster to obtain a presidential appointment, but once you had it, you owed favors to no one.

***

I took Lois Welch with me to my new FCC office, located at 12th Street and Pennsylvania Avenue, Northwest, as my Confidential Assistant. She had been with me in my early years at the FBI. When Hoover assigned me to Capitol Hill to assist the Appropriations Committee, she came over with a strong recommendation from Carmine Bellino, a close friend and associate in the Department of Justice of Robert Kennedy. Bellino later achieved fame as the investigator who "got" Jimmy Hoffa, the head of the Teamsters Union. Another of my FCC staff, Rose Marie Borda, had also worked with me on the Hill. A good friend of Lois's, she was my No. 2 "girl" -- this, remember, was long before NOW and the feminist movement. When Lois became ill and retired on disability, Rose succeeded her as my Confidential Assistant.

My position entitled me to a high-level lawyer to provide legal guidance and a skilled engineer to help me understand technical matters of broadcasting. In filling these positions I got involved in a contest for another position, that of Secretary of the Commission. Chairman Hyde had a problem here because there were two strong candidates, both of whom had important Republican support. One was Bill Campbell, a retired Army electronics expert; the other, Mary Jane Morris, said to be a close friend of Republican Party Chairman Len Hall.

To help the FCC Chairman out of his dilemma, I offered to take Campbell as my engineering assistant, leaving Hyde free to appoint Mary Jane Morris as Secretary. He was delighted with the solution. Later, when Bill left, I filled the place for Legal Assistant on my staff by employing David Williams. When David left, I replaced him with Thomas Dougherty. In fact, I was blessed with a succession of talented legal assistants after Tom departed the FCC, including Arthur Gladstone, Sidney Goldman, Peggy Reed, Jim Winston, and Frank Young.

Thus I began my tenure at the FCC, a tenure of almost twenty-eight years which included six presidential appointments by four Presidents. My last appointment, shortly before my retirement, was from President Ronald Reagan, who named me as Chairman of the Commission early in his Administration. During those nearly three decades of technological revolution in broadcasting I performed what I hope will be judged a valuable service to the American public. I am profoundly grateful for the opportunity I had to serve my country.

Bob Lee with his daughter, Patricia, mid-1950s.

11

GOSSIP AND POLITICS

No one said it would be easy, and it wasn't. And the reviews were mixed. One trade publication said that "(Commissioner Lee) remains an enigma to friends and foes alike. His record has been a series of self-contradictions."

That's the kind of assessment that makes you wonder what life is all about. Do you do the correct thing, or worry about whether or not someone agrees with you? I dedicated myself to doing the right thing, regardless of the fall-out. I wasn't dogmatic. I believe that my willingness to look at all sides of a question, without being narrow-minded enabled me to earn, and keep, the support of broadcasters and viewer advocates alike.

***

Part of the confusion evident in this trade publication comment is due to a misunderstanding of the mission of the FCC. Some people don't even have enough information to have a misunderstanding -- they don't know what the FCC is, does, or could do. During the recent bicentennial year of the Bill of Rights some pollster found that only one-third of the American people knew what the FCC is. That's bad news, but I wonder what a man-on-the-street survey would show if people were asked what the capital initials FCC stand for. One in ten maybe? Yet the FCC is charged with regulating a broad range of activities intimately affecting our everyday lives -- including the freedom of speech guaranteed by the First Amendment of the Bill of Rights.

The Communications Act of 1934, which created the FCC, pulled together tasks formerly assigned to several government departments and commissions and charged the new agency with regulating wire and wireless communications, including telephone, telegraph, radio broadcasting, and before long, television. The act has been amended many times since 1934, but its basic objectives remain the same, especially the protection of the "public interest."

Responsible to Congress, of course, since it was to carry out duties given to the national legislature by the Constitution, the FCC was nonetheless designed as an independent regulatory agency. Still, no Federal agency reliant on appropriated funds to execute its tasks can be truly independent. Federal bureaucrats often say, "The President proposes, but the Congress disposes." True enough. But though Congress may add or subtract from the President's budget proposing funding for an agency, his recommendations at least influence and shape House and Senate decisions. And, of course, it is the President who nominates members of the Commission and designates one of them as Chairman.

I'll return to some of the partisan squabbling and tug-of-war contests between the Administration and Congress over appointments, but first I should briefly explain how the FCC emerged out of the need to regulate radio broadcasting.

Anyone who has seen Ken Burns's public television production "Empire of the Air" or read Tom Lewis's book by that title has some idea of the phenomenal impact radio had on American society. How exciting it was to hear Graham McNamee describe the Washington parade welcoming the American hero Charles

Lindbergh home from his solo flight across the Atlantic; the broadcast gave a tremendous lift to the American spirit. And sharing the tension of the announcer and fans at a World Series baseball game or at ringside in a Dempsey-Tunney fight for the heavyweight title of the world brought cheers or groans in living rooms far from the action.

In the 1920s the growth of radio stations and the beginning of broadcasting networks came so fast that regulation of the airwaves broke down. Although a Federal court held that the Secretary of Commerce had the right to assign a wavelength to a station, he could not exercise discretion in the issuance of licenses. Another Federal court went further, ruling that the Radio Act of 1912 did not expressly grant the Secretary power to establish regulations; he was required to issue licenses subject only to the regulations in the Act. Many broadcasters promptly jumped their frequencies and increased their power and operating hours at will. Some responsible members of the infant radio industry, in a series of conferences, tried to achieve self-regulation, but since the Secretary of Commerce was powerless to deal with the chaotic situation, their effort failed.

Congress responded by passing the Radio Act of 1927, creating a five-member Federal Radio Commission empowered to issue station licenses, allocate frequency bands to various services, and assign specific frequencies and power to individual stations. The FRC's new rules and regulations soon forced about 150 of the existing 732 stations to give up their licenses.

The unauthorized stations of course resisted giving up their investment, but the FCC, regarding them as "pirates," actually raided and dismantled some of them. No matter that the press tabbed the raiders as "Kilocycle Kops," the Commission's action was a necessary evil, in that the illegal stations' signals caused hopeful auditors of authorized stations to hear only garbled talk. In a minor way this problem arose again with the advent of television and stations had to accommodate to the FCC's table of allocations. For example, people often ask whatever happened to VHF Channel 1, which the Commission assigned to non-broadcast users.   At least one western operator had to close down his station. My recollection is that he sued the government over the loss of a valuable property, but I doubt if he ever collected.

Under the 1927 Act jurisdiction over telephone and telegraph services remained in other departments, and the divided and sometimes overlapping authority caused a great deal of confusion. So President Franklin Roosevelt directed the Secretary of Commerce to form an interdepartmental committee to study the matter.

The committee recommended the establishment of a new agency that would regulate all interstate and foreign communication by wire and radio, including telephone, telegraph, and broadcast. Clarence Dill in the Senate and Sam Rayburn in the House introduced bills for this purpose. The main debate in Congress concerned an amendment which would have required that 25 percent of the broadcast facilities be allocated to religious, cultural, agricultural, cooperative, labor, and similar nonprofit organizations.   The defeat of this important amendment left broadcasters a great deal of freedom to follow their own course and had important implications for the future of programming -- in television as well as radio.

Besides   abolishing   the   Federal   Radio   Commission   and consolidating regulatory functions formerly performed by it, the Interstate Commerce Commission, the Post Office Department and the State Department, the 1934 Act gave the FCC additional authority over communications, including supervision of rates of interstate and international common carriers, and administration within the United States of international agreements relating to electrical communications generally.

***

By the time I joined the Commission, radio broadcasting had already enjoyed its "golden age." The new technology of television, emerging just after World War II, would profoundly affect our lives in ways that its inventors could not have imagined.

Television has proved to be the biggest bonanza since the California Gold Rush. But that wasn't obvious at first. A lot of well-informed and respected critics pointed out the obstacles the new medium had to surmount. Consider that when the first licenses were issued there were no sets capable of receiving the broadcast signal, and naturally no advertiser would purchase time if there was no visible market. Only a visionary and wellfinanced pioneer would risk the hazard of building a structure, erecting a tower, and providing programming in those early days when costs ran into the millions of dollars. He would suffer heavy losses for several years while gradually encouraging potential viewers to buy the then-grossly-overpriced television sets, and only if he could get enough of the public to buy them would advertisers show any interest. Those bold and farsighted enough to venture in this uncharted area eventually won large rewards and some of the richest people in the country owe their fortunes to this new technology.

On the other hand, some four or five skeptics in top-market cities surrendered licenses now valued at about a billion dollars each. Zenith Corporation of Chicago had a valid license for a TV channel but decided not to take the gamble on a technology it believed unable to attract advertisers. Instead, Zenith became the first advocate of subscription television, in which the viewer pays for the program just as if he were going to the theater.

The skeptics were wrong of course. Like the proliferation of radio stations in the 1920s, so did applications for television station licenses flood into the FCC in the 1940s. And just as the predecessor agency had granted AM radio broadcast licenses more or less automatically to applicants who could demonstrate they would not interfere with other stations, so did the FCC treat applicants for television licenses. In no time at all 108 licenses -- among them seven for New York City stations, seven for Los Angeles -- had been granted. Maybe one reason the Commission granted licenses so readily was that there were so many skeptics who thought the new fad wouldn't survive, that people would rather go to the movies.

Luckily, it suddenly dawned on someone at the Commission that this novelty was going to be something big and attractive. In 1948 the Commission clamped down and imposed a "freeze" on the issuance of licenses which lasted until 1952. With the freeze lifted when I came on board in 1953, the main task facing the seven commissioners and the Commission staff was making decisions on television license applications. The limited range of available VHF channels (2-13) and the necessity of ruling on equally meritorious applications which were mutually exclusive -- that is, if both were awarded, they would cancel each other out -- made for difficult choices. And, of course, the applicants often had powerful backers in the business world and in government. At a time when members of Congress and Federal officials were less concerned about the ethics of accepting or doing favors in government business than they have since become, improprieties -- or what appeared to be-occurred.

***

Some critics have concluded that the FCC became the captive of the television industry in the 1950s. They are mistaken, but there was a good deal of influence-peddling and some commissioners acted improperly.

Partisanship and the perennial jockeying for power between the legislative and executive branches of government also played their part in determining the make-up of the Commission and the members' decisions. Finally in control of the White House after long, frustrating years of Roosevelt and Truman, Republicans in the Administration wanted to reorganize the FCC and clean out the liberals.

The first task was to name a new Chairman. On this matter, there were differences in the White House. The new Chairman must be a Republican, naturally, and the obvious choice seemed to be Rosel Hyde, who was strongly supported by Broadcasting magazine. But Hyde seemed too mild, too lacking in partisan fervor, said backers of John Doerfer. At length, Hyde was named Chairman for one year -- he heard the news at home on the radio- but was told to get rid of holdover left-wingers on the staff. It was a kind of probationary appointment, and Hyde's straitlaced moral principles didn't fit him for the task party stalwarts wanted done. White House officials acted as if Doerfer was the real head of the Commission and didn't even consult Hyde on staff appointments. (I must admit I didn't understand some of the maneuvering at the time. Confusing matters about appointments to the FCC and the Federal Trade Commission are clarified by a study for the Senate Commerce Committee in the mid-1970s by two Georgetown University professors, a "Committee Print" that has had very few readers.)

Controversy over Joe McCarthy continued to affect White House decisions about the FCC and its chairmanship. In March 1954 Adlai Stevenson, Eisenhower's opponent in the 1952 presidential contest, made a televised speech denouncing McCarthy. Joe demanded equal broadcast time to reply and said he was sure the FCC would grant it. The networks granted the free time to the Republican National Committee, which instead of giving it to Joe selected Vice President Nixon to make the reply.

I endorsed the networks' action and when questioned about it, I replied, "McCarthy's my friend, but in this case it seems I would have to say, 'Look, pal, it seems like a square deal to me.'" The authors of the Senate Commerce Committee study credit my comment with being "the first public note of disagreement between the FCC and Senator McCarthy." It came on the same day that Senator Ralph Flanders, a Vermont Republican, opened the attack on McCarthy that led to his censure by the Senate in December. President Eisenhower, who had restrained himself so long in dealing with McCarthy, sent Flanders a note saying the country needed "more Republican voices like yours."

The Administration's dilemma over the FCC chairmanship continued. Sherman Adams tried to persuade Doerfer to shift to the Federal Power Commission. He refused and I wasn't interested either. Nor was Hyde. He wasn't going to continue as FCC Chairman, but his term as a commissioner still had five years to run. Then Adams tried to get George Sterling to accept the chairmanship, but he suggested that Hyde stay in the job.

Eventually Sterling was pressured off the FCC and George C. McConnaughey, a Columbus, Ohio, lawyer and a former chairman of the Ohio Public Service Commission, was sworn in as Chairman in October 1954 in Sherman Adams's office. He and Senator John Bricker were close friends. Like my appointment a year before, McConnaughey's was a recess appointment, and his association with the telephone industry -- AT&T -- caused him to face a "withering interrogation" in a hearing before Senator Magnuson's Commerce Committee. Estes Kefauver wanted to know how McConnaughey could represent the public interest in FCC regulations of telephone rates and services. He did win confirmation, however, in March 1955.

McConnaughey turned out to be a rather controversial chairman. Criticisms arose over his informal friendly dealings with the broadcast industry, and his time in office has been called the "darkest period" of FCC history. The Commission experienced heavy pressure from both political parties. The authors of the appointments study, whose judgments I think are a little too harsh, say that there was very little regulation going on in these years. They say, for example, that "McConnaughey, Doerfer, and Richard Mack emasculated an FCC staff report on AT&T and Western Electric so that it was favorable to the industry." When Frieda Hennock resigned and returned to the practice of law in New York, liberal Democrats concerned about the influence of private industry on the Commission lost a strong advocate of their cause.

Dick Mack of Florida was Frieda Hennock's replacement. His thirty-two months on the Commission contributed to its declining reputation as a defender of the public interest. An affable man whose marriage and important patrons in his home state seemed to promise him a quick rise to prominence, Mack came to the Washington scene without instruction in the ethics and proprieties of regulatory policy and procedures. His tragic FCC career demonstrates the importance of indoctrinating new appointees to Federal offices by the general counsels of their agencies and by appropriate officials of the Department of Justice.

***

The cause celebre which brought Mack's downfall and intense scrutiny of the FCC by Congress arose out of competing applications for a television channel in Miami. Mack's friend from college days, Thurman A. Whiteside, had a reputation as a "fixer," and he exerted a lot of pressure on Mack to support the application by National Airlines. Eastern Airlines was National's main rival, and one of Eastern's backers tried to get Vice President Nixon to enlist me in its behalf, an attempt I considered improper.

The Commission was closely divided and deliberated the issue for months. We reached a tentative decision to award the license to National Airlines, but it leaked out before we-made it final. Without the leak it might have been possible for commissioners to switch their votes, but the difficulty of explaining a change pretty much locked them in to the preliminary action. A contest between rival airlines for a TV channel, an awareness that Mack had been careless in his contacts with old friends and may have caved in to their influence, and the concern of powerful politicians ranged on opposite sides of the issue all stimulated demands for an airing of the Commission's work on the case.

Before we took final action, Senator Magnuson called the seven commissioners to appear for a hearing on what seemed a barely plausible matter. After the pro forma public meeting, he asked us to step into his office. There we were confronted by a Florida Senator who was not even a member of Magnuson's Commerce Committee. Although he had never publicly avowed his wish that the license be granted to Eastern Airlines, he now made an outrageous proposal to that effect. I protested that the vote had been taken and it would be improper to change it because a United States Senator wanted us to. The Commission should have made a public record of this incident, but I do not believe it ever did.

Soon after that exchange we voted to award Channel 10 in Miami to National Airlines. Mack cast one of the four favorable votes. In later hearings before a House oversight subcommittee Mack made a very poor showing. The public hearings on the Miami case disclosed the close ties between Mack and Whiteside, and some of Mack's critics believed that he may even have sold his vote. Chairman Oren Harris (D, Arkansas) suggested to the anguished witness that he ought to resign from the Commission. The White House was embarrassed by the investigation, and Sherman Adams demanded Mack's resignation "at once." Mack gave in to the demand. (Ironically, Adams himself was later accused of using his influence to get favorable treatment for a New England textile manufacturer, and though exonerated, felt compelled to resign.) John S. Cross, a witty engineer who was nominated to replace Mack, is reported to have said, "I may not be too smart, but I'm awfully clean."

Mack had clearly allowed friendship and improper influence to sway his decision, but to his credit there was no indication that he had ever received any personal profits from National Airlines' advocates. Rather, he simply conducted himself in the same manner as he had in his earlier role as a member of the Florida Railroad and Public Utilities Commission. He and Whiteside were indicted but the indictment was later dropped. Whiteside committed suicide, and in 1963 Dick Mack's body was found on a sheetless bed in a skid row flophouse. On the floor were two stacks of nickels and pennies totaling forty cents. The young man with bright prospects was divorced by his wife and became a confirmed alcoholic. I attended his funeral in Arlington National Cemetery where he was buried with full military honors.

***

While the Miami case was hanging fire in the Commission, other controversial matters came to the attention of our overseers on Capitol Hill. The Senate -- and later the House -inquired into the rumors about political influence being exerted during an FCC comparative hearing for a television channel at Fresno, California. The case had lingered in deadlock for a long time. I finally wrote a concurring opinion that awarded the license by a 4-2 vote. I indicated my belief that it was time to resolve the case; I was more concerned that the public get the service it needed than I was with the respective merits of the applicants. Either of them could do a creditable job. Long-drawn-out contests like this one where rival contestants seemed equally qualified led me to believe that we might as well draw the winner out of a hat by lottery rather than quibble endlessly over picayune details.

There was a lot of gossip about the case and some high-powered political maneuvering that I wasn't aware of. I did receive a call on behalf of one of the applicants from Representative John

Phillips, an old friend from my days on the Hill. I told him I would not talk about the case and then hung up the phone. He was angry then but thanked me later, because if I had listened to his plea and written a memorandum of our conversation, as I was required to do, it would have come to light in a subsequent congressional investigation.

My involvement in the case came up first in the summer of 1956 when Senate staffers tried to implicate me in some sort of fix. Besides alleging that Vice President Nixon had discussed the case with me, they claimed that his political friend Murray Chotiner had sought to influence me. Fortunately, I had never met Chotiner and he did not contact me.

The Senate Investigations Committee, suspecting payoffs by the winning applicant, pursued the matter for several months in 1956. A friend of mine from FBI days, Carmine Bellino, and Robert F. Kennedy, the committee's counsel, interviewed my legal assistant, Dave Williams, at some length, trying to find out if Nixon or Chotiner had approached me and whether Dave had heard any of the "common talk around the Commission" about a sale of the license and asserting that "anyone who hadn't heard it must be deaf." Dave replied, "I must be deaf." Kennedy and Bellino then interviewed me. Apparently they were finally satisfied there had been no hanky panky, and to their credit they refused to give their files to other individuals intent on smearing me and other commissioners.

***

Questions about the Fresno case and other FCC decisions didn't end with the Senate inquiry conducted by Kennedy and Bellino. They came up again the next year in a House investigation, which apparently originated out of a visit from Commissioner Bartley, one of the dissenters in the Miami case, to his uncle Speaker Sam Rayburn. With the Speaker's support, the House Interstate and

Foreign Commerce Committee began to take a deep interest in the Commission and the commissioners personally. The committee members had been hearing a lot of gossip about "fixed" cases, and I had been involved in some of the stories. An unsuccessful applicant for the Miami license apparently was responsible for many of the rumors reaching the committee.

In the summer of 1957 the House Oversight Committee employed a New York University law professor, Bernard Schwartz, as counsel to investigate the Commission. Chairman Morgan M. Moulder, a Missouri Democrat, gave Schwartz full support. I anticipated a fair, nonpartisan inquiry and welcomed it at first. But Schwartz turned out to be an egotistical, ambitious, brash young man who couldn't get along with anyone. Since he didn't like the way the committee was handling some of his evidence, he arranged to leak it to the New York Times, where it appeared as a front-page expose. Just as eager to uncover political influence on the Commission by White House officials and members of Congress as by private business, he soon made committee members uneasy and they finally fired him. Even out of the job, however, he stayed on in Washington, continuing to press his charges in testifying before the Oversight Committee, now chaired by Oren Harris, an Arkansas Democrat.

I appeared before the Committee on March 31, 1958, and was questioned at length about who had paid the bills on various official trips I had taken. The members found no improprieties and gave me a clean bill of health.

A few days before my questioning, my old enemy Drew Pearson devoted a whole column to me. He dredged up musty charges about my giving the names of State Department security risks to McCarthy and my wife's and my part in the Maryland senatorial campaign for John Marshall Butler; my reward for these "two pieces of backstage business," he said, had been the appointment to the FCC. On a matter more pertinent to the committee's investigation, he said I had reversed my opinion on the Fresno case because of Murray Chotiner's intervention and on a Jacksonville, Florida, case because of a plea from a prominent Catholic cleric. These and other of his smears were demonstrably wrong; he had me casting favorable votes when in fact I dissented. I wrote a long letter to the <u>Washington Post</u> detailing Pearson's inaccuracies, but my advisers talked me out of sending it.

Some amusing matters came from the investigation. Investigators trailing rumors about favors to Sherman Adams from his industrialist friend Bernard Goldfine found they had registered at a Plymouth, Massachusetts, hotel with one Robert E. Lee. Assuming Lee was the FCC commissioner, they rushed back to Washington to tell Oren Harris. Neither the White House nor Pearson's associate Jack Anderson could verify my meeting with them, and Harris sent the sleuths back to Plymouth to check, just to be sure. Now they discovered that Robert E. Lee was Goldfine's black chauffeur. Oren Harris told me the story later. If he had only checked with me at the time, I could have saved the investigators a return trip to Plymouth and the taxpayers a fair amount of travel money. But this is Washington.

Another amusing incident concerned colored television sets which had been given to the commissioners by RCA -- a favor of course but also a means of demonstrating an important new technology. When the investigators learned about the sets, the committee called all of the commissioners to testify about the matter. The amusing aspect of the incident was the fact that the serviceman who delivered the set to our house showed my wife the receipt he had been given by Oren Harris who had received an identical set the same day. (Harris returned it to RCA the day the hearings began.)

The color television sets we received I considered to be on loan for the purpose of bringing us up to date on what is now termed "state-of-the-art" equipment and in that sense a means of helping us tarry out our public duties.   Similarly, in my years on the Commission I had other broadcasting equipment installed in my home that was the property of the FCC or essential to the performance of my job.   For example, the Department of Defense insisted that Civil Defense required the placing of a two-way automobile radio in the FCC's car.   But the Commission didn't have a car.   Since I was the Defense Commissioner, it was decided that the radio should be installed in my car.   Before I would authorize its installation, I asked the Defense Coordinator to get a ruling from the Judge Advocate General, which he did.   When I bought a new car and switched the radio, I had to spend my own money to repair the hole for the antenna in my old car.

Although I came out of both the Senate and House investigations untainted by scandal, two of my fellow commissioners were less fortunate.   I've already told Dick Mack's troubles.   John Doerfer's were somewhat different but they helped bring his downfall too.

Doerfer admitted accepting travel and hotel expenditures from the broadcasting industry and getting honoraria for speeches.   Those lapses, some of which I think were mere oversights on his part, were considered fairly minor at that time, and I believed the committee was making a mountain out of a mole hill.   He was a stubborn Dutchman, though, and went beyond the bounds of discretion in fighting back.

***

When a scandal erupted in the late 1950s over rigged TV quiz shows -- portrayed in a recent PBS broadcast and described in a book by Kent Anderson -- many outraged viewers demanded that the FCC crack down on the networks by investigating their programming policies.   Chairman Doerfer insisted that the First Amendment and the Communications Act prohibited censorship; the agency was powerless to investigate.   Oren Harris thought otherwise.

The two had a public confrontation before a large audience when Harris made a speech to the National Association of Broadcasters. After Harris's criticisms of the broadcasters' laxity, Doerfer rose to defend them.   Disregarding the amenities of attacking a distinguished guest speaker, but to thunderous applause, he excoriated Harris and defended the networks. A few of us there knew it was an awful mistake. Harris had a pretty short fuse and was bound to react.

Not long after that episode the New York Herald Tribune told -- probably thanks to Harris's investigators -- that a prominent Miami broadcaster, George Storer, had entertained Doerfer and his wife on his yacht. In fact, this wasn't the first time it happened and come to light. They had been friends for several years and I'm sure John, a good and kindly gentleman in my book, thought he was doing nothing wrong, certainly nothing venal. I too had been entertained by George Storer and I played golf with him both before and after this incident. But he had a substantial interest before the Commission and the appearance of impropriety can be damaging. It was to John.

When Doerfer was called before Harris's committee he insisted that people had no right to expect him "to live like a hermit." But the Washington Post got after him and Eisenhower's appointments secretary agreed that he was guilty of ethical lapses and ought to resign. Acting on bad advice or simply impetuously, he asked to see the President. After that visit he agreed to write his letter of resignation and bring it to the White House at once. A heavy snow storm prevented his delivering the letter, whereupon the White House dispatched a car equipped with tire chains to pick it up.

***

Meanwhile I was up for reappointment. My term would expire on June 30, 1960. But 1960 was a presidential election year and there was little chance that a Democratic Senate, hoping to win back the White House, would confirm me, especially if I should be named Chairman, as seemed likely with Doerfer's resignation imminent. So I visited my mentor Senator Bridges and explained my problem. I asked him to call the White House to tell them I wasn't interested in the chairmanship. While we were talking he got a call from Doerfer, snowbound at home, still reluctant to submit his promised resignation letter; he asked Senator Bridges to intercede on his behalf at the White House. In my presence, the Senator indicated that he felt there was little he could do since Doerfer had offered to resign. That same day the White House car plowed through the snow to John's residence, dooming his hope of staying on the Commission. He ended up in Miami as vice president of the Storer Broadcasting Company.

I don't know whether Senator Bridges passed on my message to the White House, but I assume he did because I got a call that afternoon from Jerry Morgan, counsel to the President, telling me of the President's intention to name Frederick W. Ford to replace Doerfer as Chairman.

I was renominated but the confirmation dragged on for months. My case got entangled with the renomination of Earl Kintner to the Federal Trade Commission. Some Democrats on the Hill seemed bent on holding off action on both of us until after the election, though Senator Magnuson's committee reported favorably on me by a unanimous vote while tabling action on Kintner.

Luckily for me, I had good friends on the Hill in both parties. Bridges spoke to his Democratic colleague Senator Kerr, who in turn urged Majority Leader Lyndon Johnson to support my nomination. Before long I heard that I was going to be the only presidential appointee confirmed before the election.

Kintner, a fine and able man, knew of my strength on the Hill and talked to me several times indicating we must stick together. I had to handle a difficult problem tactfully, since I had been told by people in a position to know that I would be the notable exception -- the one Republican nominee to either commission to be confirmed by a Democratic Senate.

Again there was a debate on the Senate floor. William Proxmire of Wisconsin and Ernest Gruening of Alaska, both Democrats, spoke against reconfirming me; Styles Bridges and Everett Dirksen of Illinois argued strongly for my reappointment. Dirksen told his colleagues he had examined my record in detail and had asked me a lot of questions in a face-to-face interview.

Despite the evident displeasure of some Democratic Senators with the recent conduct of some of my colleagues, I won reappointment on June 23, 1960, on a roll call vote of 64 to 19. I felt sorry for Kintner, but I needed the job and was pleased to have it renewed.

12

THE PUBLIC INTEREST

I came to the Federal Communications Commission so green I thought a "frequency" had to do with the interval between drinks. Dreading to reveal my technical ignorance at my confirmation hearing, I bought a book on elementary electricity, which, sad to say, I still don't understand. But my almost twenty-eight years on the FCC gave me an education on the responsibilities of citizenship and of protecting the public interest.

I believed in 1953, as I do now, that free enterprise in business and industry provides our best hope of achieving a good society. The public interest is well served when government restraints are kept to a minimum. In my long career on the FCC, I was guided by those ideas and continued to trust that business competition would result in the greatest social benefits. But I also learned that when the broadcasting industry's efforts at self-regulation fail, government intervention becomes necessary. When, for example, the FCC was flooded with complaints -- and program transcripts -- showing from twelve to twenty-two commercial interruptions of a half-hour television program, I believed we had a duty to correct that kind of programming.

As I related earlier, competition for television station licenses is hardly an unmixed blessing when the endless delays occasioned by arguments over the right choice prevent a needed service to the public. When the FCC, in 1952, announced the lifting of the long freeze, it met in an unusual all-night session and granted uncontested applications probably to avoid competing applications and the ordeal of years of hearings.

***

The first license granted after that session was to a station in Austin, Texas, and the applicant was Senator Lyndon B. Johnson. My Republican friends complained to me that there was some kind of fix. But when I investigated, I found a simple explanation: The applications were granted in alphabetical order and Austin, Texas, was first on the list. Not that LBJ was averse to using his influence on the FCC and on the broadcasting industry. As his party's leader and a member of the Commerce Committee, FCC's oversight committee, he didn't hesitate to use his power. Controversy swirled about the Johnson broadcasting interests for years, but Lyndon claimed he had nothing to do with the operation of the stations -- they were his wife's business, not his. When he became President, Lady Bird Johnson put the family broadcasting stock in trusteeship, but suspicions of conflict of interest continued, including his influence over FCC actions.

Clearly Lyndon Johnson abused his position, though not necessarily at the FCC. One network president told me that Lyndon would call him to Washington now and then and tell him what programs he wanted aired on his station. The networks accommodated him; a Johnson UHF station had the affiliation of all three networks, an historical first. A competing VHF station complained bitterly about this "monopoly" but to no avail, and ultimately the Johnsons made a deal closing their UHF station and acquiring a 50 percent interest in the VHF station. FCC was on the hot seat and many people believed the "independent" agency, some of whose commissioners hoped for reappointment, failed to protect the public interest. But everyone prospered, and the FCC took the position that it was approving business judgments in accordance with free-enterprise principles.

Lyndon Johnson never attempted to influence me, and I owe my third term on the FCC to a reappointment by this Democratic President. I'll tell that story later.

***

The "monopoly" question often confronted the FCC when a newspaper sought to add a radio or television station to its holdings. Although I agreed with the idea that a community should enjoy a diversity of views from the local media, I also believed that the survival of newspapers was a public good and that ownership of a television station could provide the revenue to keep a newspaper from folding; and if it folded, the city's rival paper would then enjoy a print monopoly. Witness what happened in Washington, D.C., where the Post owned a television station but its morning rival, the Times-Herald, did not. And like many afternoon papers with the advent of television, the venerable Washington Evening Star finally gave up the ghost. The Post has a competitor now, but its losses cost the Rev. Moon's Unification Church millions of dollars every year.

One contest for ownership of a television station by a Boston newspaper, the Herald Traveler, dragged on for seventeen years. One attorney I know collected enough fees from it to put his kids through college. Sterling "Red" Quinlan detailed the story in The Hundred Million Dollar Lunch, a title based on a luncheon of a Herald Traveler editor and the FCC chairman, an ex parte affair that eventually cost the newspaper ownership of the television station.

The Commission awarded the station to the Herald Traveler -- twice, as I recall -- but the ex parte allegations forced us to reconsider. Eventually there were only four Commissioners qualified to vote on the matter without starting the whole procedure over. I could have frustrated my colleagues by failing to vote, but if I didn't participate I would have forced Chairman Hyde to vote, who had a good reason for not doing so. I knew, too, that if he voted, the decision would be the same. Rather than deferring the decision another year or more, I cast my dissenting vote and the Herald Traveler lost. As I predicted in my dissent, Boston ended up with one less newspaper. When the freeze on TV station licenses ended, the FCC adopted frequency criteria and a new allocation table intended to provide nationwide television service. The available VHF channels (2-13) were too few to meet the criteria, and so additional channels in the UHF band (14-83) were provided. The Commissioners made a serious mistake, however. Assuming that the new channels would be competitive with the existing ones, they assigned both types to the same communities. But manufacturers of television sets were reluctant to go to the expense and time of converting at the assembly line to a set capable of receiving all VHF and UHF channels. The FCC tried to encourage the manufacture of a device enabling the viewer to switch from one frequency to the other. When these attempts failed, we reluctantly, but successfully, asked the Congress for legislation providing that all television sets shipped in interstate commerce be capable of receiving both VHF and UHF.

We did a lot of head scratching and fumbling, though, before we reached that solution.

***

I devoted most of my working time on the FCC to the problem of making UHF broadcasting compatible with VHF. I am proud of the title bestowed on me rather facetiously by my introducers on speech-making occasions as "Mr. UHF." I believe that if I had not led the Commission on this matter, UHF broadcasting would be dead, since there were competitors who claimed they could put this space on the spectrum to more productive use.

My first idea was to require all television broadcasting to be in the UHF portion of the spectrum and leave the VHF space to other users. But when I broached this solution, protests poured in from vested interests clinging to a valuable franchise and the notion had to be abandoned. We also made a feeble attempt to reserve the UHF channels for the new technology of color television but this also died aborning.

Next we tried "de-intermixture." This was a plan to make one market area exclusively VHF, another all UHF. But owners of entrenched VHF stations complained that the FCC was about to ruin them, and the Congress, especially the Senate Commerce Committee, heard their pleas and blocked that solution. If only VHF hadn't got a head start, all television might have been allocated to UHF, but it was too late to apply that remedy.

Besides the lack of a television set capable of receiving both VHF and UHF broadcasts, some of our engineers contended that UHF would not work well in large cities or in rugged terrain because signals would bounce off tall buildings or mountains. But, encouraged by one of our engineers, I asked my fellow Commissioners to try a practical experiment. Why not put up a UHF station in New York City and find out if it would work? If it worked there, it would work anyplace. They were rather cool to the idea but at least told me I might go ahead on my own and try to get funds from the Bureau of the Budget and the Congress. Much to the surprise of my colleagues my presentations to the Bureau and the Hill resulted in an appropriation of two million dollars for an experimental UHF station in New York on a temporary basis.

The project was assigned to me and it proved to be my most interesting FCC experience. I talked to radio station WNYC in New York, and we agreed that the tower should be placed on the

Empire State Building where the other existing stations were located. I had considerable trouble getting clearances from unions to use the other stations' programs -- we weren't interested in the programs, only what happened to the signal-but they were very cooperative in waiving rules that might impede the experiment because they saw that in the long range its success would create more stations and more jobs for their members.

Who could we get to run the station? Well, why not the City of New York itself, which could use the station for ambulance services, police line-ups, and other functions as well as broadcasts of the VHF stations' programs? The person in charge of radio station WNYC was enthusiastic about the idea, and when we went on the air as WUHF, he made a great success out of it. We made arrangements with the U.S. Census Bureau to locate particular sites to test reception, and we asked people to let us install all-channel sets in their houses and apartments. We had eight of these sets custom made and we kept moving them from apartment to apartment. At the end of a three-year test, our engineers found that when outdoor antennas were used, there was no significant difference in the UHF and VHF signals. The result proved a great boon for the promotion of UHF broadcasting.

Now that the experiment had ended, the FCC had an obligation to tear down the tower. What a shame! Then it dawned on us that we could save the station, and the cost of destruction, by giving it to the City of New York. We did so at a ceremony at Gracie Mansion, and Mayor Bill O'Dwyer gave me an award. WUHF became WNYC and remains on the air today.

The success of WUHF provided impetus for the legislation requiring that all television sets manufactured for sale in interstate commerce be capable of receiving all broadcast signals. FCC Chairman Newton Minnow was instrumental in persuading Congress to pass that important measure.

***

One of the great social advances coming out of the new allocation table adopted after the lifting of the freeze was the reservation of channels for educational television. The main credit for this achievement belongs to the first woman Commissioner, Frieda Hennock. She fought hard against commercial interests for some modest allocations in major television markets, and later increases have made this alternative to commercial programs widely available. Originally ETV was intended to provide in-school instruction in elementary schools, and many school systems subscribed to the service. That kind of television has largely disappeared, and stations providing educational programs, pleading their need for money, persuaded the FCC to allow them a limited amount of "institutional advertising," which gives credit to the organization providing program funds. I fear the next step will make these stations almost fully commercial, giving us too many of that type and abandoning Frieda Hennock's dream of enlivening instruction for children in city ghettos or the hills of Appalachia.

***

One of the knottiest problems faced by the FCC is known as the "fairness doctrine." When radio and television broadcasts began to appear as powerful influences on public attitudes, Congress became concerned -- lest listeners and viewers be brainwashed. Its first concern was political broadcasting, and it passed legislation providing that if a candidate for office was sold or given time to present his views, then his opponent should have an opportunity to state his. There has been a long running battle over this doctrine, and broadcasters -- primarily the networks -- fought it; they argued that because of the First Amendment's free speech guarantee they were not required to give both sides of an issue. They succeeded in getting the law amended so that it became ambiguous, difficult to administer, and essentially invalid.

In 1987, the FCC repealed the fairness doctrine.

Frankly, I thought the fairness doctrine worked pretty well, and I think it is unfortunate that the networks hid behind the First Amendment. Still, the average broadcaster has continued to adhere to the doctrine out of a sense of decency. Many broadcasters, especially small ones, have indicated to me that it was a lot easier for them under the old rule to justify putting an unpopular position on the air because they could blame the government requirement. Now that fairness is discretionary, it becomes more difficult for them to justify their position. For example, one broadcaster in a small town told me of his dilemma when his brother-in-law ran for mayor. His wife, ignorant of the FCC's fairness requirement, prodded him to help her brother by disparaging his opponent. He could then tell her about the danger of losing his license; if his wife's brother ran now, he might end up in divorce court if he tried to be fair.

In every election year since radio broadcasting began in 1920 there have been controversies over providing equal time for the presentation of opposing views. The advent of television greatly heated up the argument because the visual medium and slick -- sometimes dirty -- advertisements often proved decisive in political campaigns. Section 326 of the Communications Act of 1934 forbade censorship by broadcasters, and for many years that provision left them vulnerable to libel suits. Each of the fifty states of the Union has dealt with the problem of libel by specific, though of course not uniform, legislation. The dilemma of preserving the constitutional guarantee of free speech and at the same time imposing self-protective limits will surely continue to plague legislatures, broadcasters, and the FCC.

One important Supreme Court case, known as Red Lion, dealt with this issue in 1969 (Red Lion Broadcasting Co. v. Federal Communications Commission 395 U.S. 367, 89 S.Ct. 1794). The case arose out of a radio broadcast attacking the author of a book denouncing Barry Goldwater, the Republican nominee for the presidency against Lyndon Johnson in 1964. The station refused the author's demand for free equal time to reply. The FCC ruled that the broadcast was a personal attack on the book's author and that the station had failed to meet its obligation under the fairness doctrine. The Supreme Court upheld that application of the fairness doctrine, and also the FCC's new regulations growing out of the case, as a valid exercise of the Commission's authority. Reviewing the history of the doctrine, the Court held that Congress had given the FCC a broad power "to assure that broadcasters operate in the public interest," and the licensing system established by the Communications Act of 1934 was a proper exercise of the Congress's power to regulate commerce. If a station fails to meet the standard established by the act -- that a licensee should benefit "the public interest, convenience, and necessity" -- it is not a denial of free speech if the FCC fails to grant or renew a license to the station.

In the early part of my career on the FCC, I was quite sympathetic to the networks' plea to abolish the fairness doctrine. But I began to change my mind when I saw some specific abuses of the privilege. Many TV viewers may remember a newscast in which a photographer recreated -- that is, faked -- the handing-over of an attache case, thus giving an appearance of spies at work. There have been other dramatic concocted events. For example, a CBS broadcast of "Hunger in America" showed a baby said to be dying of hunger; Texas Congressman Henry Gonzales proved that in fact the baby was healthy and well cared for, a fact the network failed to acknowledge. Other CBS fabrications occurred in a program called "The Selling of the Pentagon" and in a depiction of an apparently spontaneous "pot" party of a group of students in Chicago. The Commission, after reviewing the evidence on these CBS programs, used a lot of harsh words against the network but failed to take any definitive action, saying that it was leaning over backward to protect the broadcasters' First Amendment rights.

I predict that the fairness doctrine will be re-imposed after the television audience finally gets tired of this kind of deception.

There will always be controversy over the degree of censorship the Federal government should exercise over what goes on the air. Pornography and obscenity as viewed from the Bible Belt are poles apart from the way they are seen from San Francisco's North Beach. From its inception the FCC has been bombarded with complaints about radio and television programming, especially its effect on children.

The Communications Act of 1934 originally prohibited the utterance over the air of any material that was profane, indecent, or obscene. But the act also explicitly forbids censorship of radio broadcasting, and by extension, of course, television. The FCC has had a difficult time trying to reconcile these two contradictory provisions and of reaching acceptable definitions of prohibited matter. Lawyers on both sides have done a lucrative business.

Although some judges have leaned toward the doctrinaire opinion that the First Amendment's guarantee of free speech is an absolute right, I would certainly agree with the Supreme Court justice who said there is no right to shout "Fire!" in a crowded theater. When I consider the powerful effect radio and television can have on the listening and viewing audience-especially impressionable children -- I believe there should be limitations on what is uttered and shown by the media.

***

Driving to work at the FCC one morning in the 1960s, I had what I thought was a brilliant way to solve our dilemma about censorship. I heard on the car radio a nasty disk jockey tell about the jailing of some Gulf of Mexico shrimp fishermen for their offensive language over a ship-to-shore radio. Almost no one heard them but his same kind of talk was heard by thousands.

My lawyer and I agreed that if we could get the FCC to fine some station for using foul language and if the station refused to pay the fine, then a Federal court would have to rule on what is profane or obscene.

It was a great idea, we thought. And we thought we had struck gold when an educational radio station broadcast a taped interview with the leader of the Grateful Dead in which he used the F-word and the S-word repeatedly; the case for levying a fine seemed ideal, since the station had plenty of time to check the tape before the broadcast. The FCC imposed a fine all right, but only of $100 because the station did educational broadcasting and had little money. Our hoped-for court test evaporated when the station paid the fine.

Next my staff and I drafted the "dirtiest document in FCC history," listing the words and expressions that must not be broadcast. And when a woman on a radio call-in talk show described graphically how her husband persuaded her to perform oral sex, the Commission fined the station $1,000 and anticipated a court trial after a refusal to pay the fine. We were fated to be disappointed again because the fine was paid.

Finally the test came in 1973 after a noncommercial Pacifica Broadcasting station in New York played an album in which a comedian talked at length about the "seven dirty words" which were never supposed to be used on television. The resulting case lasted five years before the Supreme Court agreed with the FCC that a daytime broadcast of those words was inappropriate. But we didn't ban their use after midnight. Still, anyone who watches some of the British imports shown on public television programs now hears the F- and S-words and sees bare breasts during prime time. And on a recent Bill Moyers "Hate on Trial" program, a racist bigot translated for the jury and the TV audience the initials "M.F." he had used in one of his tracts.

I doubt that my thoughts about this never-ending debate over free speech and censorship will bring comfort to either side. But I do get mighty irritated when some broadcasters proclaim their "freedom" just after filing complaints about "unfair competition" from other stations; or when they declare they are being treated as "second-class citizens" immediately after their licenses have been renewed. Your citizenship can't get any more "firster" than it does when you are handed a license to broadcast. Lawyers representing the communications media remember the rights of freedom of speech and press but often forget the First Amendment's other guarantees: free exercise of religion, the right to assemble peaceably, and the right "to petition the Government for a redress of grievances."

The Federal government can't deny a broadcaster his right of free speech. He can go to a public park and shout his convictions to the heavens. He has the free speech right of every citizen. To the communications lawyer who says "That's not what I mean; I'm talking about the government's restrictions on the broadcaster," I respond, "Nobody forced your client to apply for the special privilege of using the public domain, to demonstrate to the FCC that the issuance of that license would benefit the public interest, convenience, and necessity."

I have come reluctantly to the conclusion that my friends in broadcasting -- much like those in transportation, securities, energy, and defense contracting -- want to have things both ways. They accept the benefits that society confers on all citizens and then demand special privileges without any of the accompanying responsibilities. A "right" can't be regulated; a "privilege" can.

One of my predecessors on the FCC, the late Clifford Durr, turned down a second term on the Commission and told reporters: "I get so weary of having good people come before us and ask, please, to be allowed to serve the public. A few years later, the same folks return in chauffeured limousines, demanding that the

FCC keep its nose out of their free enterprise." I was luckier than Durr. I left the Commission with my respect and affection for most broadcasters still intact. But as for their attorneys? Maybe, I often thought, Shakespeare's rabble-rouser had the right idea: "First, let's kill off all the lawyers."

Words and expressions that used to shock genteel folk are now bandied about freely in polite conversation. Newspapers and serious magazines have altered their style manuals to allow the printing of four-letter words once beyond the pale. The FCC has also become more liberal in this respect. Just as state officials have to guard against tricksters trying to slip off-color words onto personalized automobile license plates, so did the Commission during my tenure prohibit station call letters that would have a connotation of indecency (e.g., WSEX, WFUK). There seems to be little attempt now to bar the use of call letters I consider offensive.

Although, as I indicated earlier, the FCC attempted in the past to get clearer instruction from the courts on definitions of obscene and profane language, they have been leery of attacking the issue directly. However, the FCC's problem has been eased in that the prohibition against the use of offensive language has now been lifted from the Communications Act and placed in the U.S. Criminal Code and made subject to fine and/or imprisonment. So far as I know there have been no convictions. The First Amendment still impedes successful prosecution of offenders.

It has become increasingly difficult to agree upon and to apply a national standard on obscene, indecent, and profane language that should not be allowed in broadcasts. I continue to believe that the Supreme Court's Red Lion decision holds profound significance. It resolved a long-continued argument as to the jurisdiction of the FCC on the question of general program format. In effect, it upheld the Commission's proposition that there is a responsibility not only on the part of the licensees but also of the regulators to have a concern for the debasing of the language used in broadcasts.

Such hotly debated questions as indecency coming over the airwaves -- or the use of taxpayers' money to support "performance artists" by the National Endowment for the Arts -- won't be settled for all time by the courts. On the Commission during my tenure, we often relied on our lawyers for advice. But we also depended on common sense in trying to wind our way through the opposite views of cultural permissiveness represented, say, by Archie Bunker and his son-in-law, "Meathead." An ability to give a fair hearing to opposing points of view should be one of the main qualifications a President should look for in appointing a person to the FCC.

***

In addition to my duties as commissioner, I was often asked to represent the United States at international conferences on telecommunications. Usually, I headed the delegation, and would be away from my commission work for weeks at a time. Sometimes I participated in votes on the commission via telephone in between sessions. My international work took me to conferences in Geneva, France, Spain, the Netherlands, Japan, China, Argentina, and Canada. For instance, I attended the 1971 Space Conference in Geneva as Vice Chairman of the U.S. Delegation. In 1973, I again returned to Geneva as Chairman of the U.S. Delegation to the Telephone and Telegraph Conference. In that same year I was the Vice Chairman of a delegation that attended the Plenipotentiary Conference in Torremolinos, Spain. In 1974, I was Chairman of our delegation to the World Administrative Radio Conference for Maritime, again in Geneva. And, in 1977, I was the Chairman of the delegation to the World Administrative Radio Conference for Broadcast Satellites, in Geneva once more.

I was also once asked to undertake a delicate mission to Yugoslavia to meet with a Soviet telecommunications minister prior to an international conference. My job was to smooth the way for acceptance of a treaty that allocated specific spectrum bands to various countries. There was much concern that the USSR would object to the treaty. Since I had a reputation as an easy-going guy who got along well with the Soviets, I was asked to fly over, gain acceptance of our position (which I did), and come back. It was whirlwind trip that gave me fresh appreciation for the shuttle diplomacy of the Henry Kissingers of this world.

Frankly, I did get along pretty well with the other delegates. Each of us would read our official statements, sometimes winking at each other, as when the Soviets would denounce the United States, or when our country pinched the politics of Cuba or Poland. Usually, the delegates would gather for drinks at a reception after a session, talk and laugh together, and become pretty good friends. One of the biggest jokes was telling each other how bitterly, and with what vituperation, we would read our public statements, as in "Tomorrow I'm going to call you a fascist capitalist, fueled by the greed of Wall Street and the Rockefellers. What do you think about that? Ha ha." As far as I could tell, none of us took the denunciations, which on this level and topic were relatively few and far between, personally. Some of the delegates didn't even take that sort of thing seriously. And more persuasion and work was accomplished at the receptions anyway, where we weren't quoted and we could talk informally.

In fact, after I left public service in 1981, I was asked to be a delegate to the 1983 Geneva World Administrative Conference for Broadcast Satellites. Unfortunately, our government did not foresee the need for a reception to honor the delegates from other countries. Since I knew how important these gatherings were for professional courtesy and deal-making, I asked several private observers to kick in some cash for a blow-out. Just to let you know how vital these gatherings are to the success of a conference, I even came across with a substantial wad to make it a go. And it went -- a very successful meeting of the minds. People still talk about that party, and how instrumental it was to the conference.

You see, these conferences are part politics, part social functions, part dire necessity. The advent of global telecommunications made cooperation a necessity. Whether we liked it or not, we needed to prevent overlap of spectrum use, coordination of spectrum allocation between and within each country, regulation of satellite availability and use, and many other of the nuts and bolts difficulties produced by a technological revolution that could not be stopped by political boundaries or ideological divisions. Today you see the result of this cooperation, in which I hope I had a hand: most countries have telephone and facsimile access to all other countries, many countries use satellite broadcasts, all countries have access to satellite programming (such as CNN and TBS), and a closer sense of community with people in other countries.

"The Boss": Commissioner Lee, in his office at the FCC.

All smiles aboard the Robert E. Lee.

13

RELIGIOUS BROADCASTING

Religious broadcasting is a serious, sensitive topic -- one that deserves its own examination.

I believe in the constitutional separation of church and state. This does not mean that I am not deeply appreciative of the Roman Catholic Church. As an Irishman and a Roman Catholic by birth and choice, my religious heritage is very important to me. It has shaped and defined my life. It has been an ever-present, constant influence -- a companion through good times and bad. I have participated in the mysterious sacraments of baptism, confirmation, and marriage. While I didn't make it to church every Sunday, and perhaps I wasn't the most humble or saintly of men, I have been, and remain, in my heart a believer in God's power and mercy. In one way or another, my faith in Jesus and my support of the Catholic Church have been constant. When I was made a Knight of Malta, it was one of the most extraordinary and deeply fulfilling moments in my life. It was an overwhelming honor, and one of which I am so very proud.

However, I have never been one to overtly flaunt my faith. While I am often very public with many parts of my life, I prefer to keep quiet counsel with my faith. It is too personal and too private to easily or comfortably share with others.

Of course, I never made a professional or governmental decision because it would benefit organized religion. But I also was not hostile to organized religion while at the FBI, as an investigator for the Congress, or as a Commissioner at the FCC. My faith guided my morality but not my authority. Frankly, it simply wasn't a factor because it just wasn't relevant to our work. That is the wonderful aspect about our government. The "big shots" can be Catholic, Protestant, Mormon, Jewish, Islamic, Hindi, Buddhist, Atheist, or Agnostic. But the Constitution promises that there will not be a state religion, and the practice of government offers wide latitude for moral decision-making, but little latitude for favoritism for a particular religion.

***

When I think of religious broadcasting and the many complex issues that surface in any discussion of this topic, I am reminded of the way we describe our forbearers -- those who settled this great country and forged many of the precepts by which we order our lives. These people were humble, but in their humility there was no weakness. Instead, that humility was tempered by boldness, and that boldness begot strength.

In that era, if we had lived then, men of the cloth might have been carrying the word of God in a horse and wagon, perhaps settling the West. They may have endured the taunts of those robust, hard-living settlers, seeking an audience of two or three, maybe twenty -- and probably passing a battered hat for a few alms to keep blood and bone together.

Imagine this possibility -- one day, as a minister was riding down a dusty road, the skies opened and a mighty voice literally surrounded him, filling the atmosphere.

"Preacher man," the voice said. "Harken unto me. I have watched you struggling day after day to carry my word to a few people in this vast land. I am well pleased, preacher man, and I am going to give you a gift to help you carry on your work. Here is a microphone."

"A what?"

"A microphone to carry the sermon of love to all the people of the Earth. I charge you to use this gift in God's name to preach love to all people of all lands. This is my gift to you. It is not an instrument for <u>profit</u>. You must account to me for its use or abuse."

At that moment -- in his total bafflement -- the minister probably would have sought assurance that such a miracle could come to pass, that words could be carried by whatever means over great distances to many more people than one person could possibly see in a lifetime. The minister might well have doubted the promise of so great a miracle. But, once the miraculous microphone was in his hands, the minister would not take long to put it to the test.

The minister would be excited at first that he could send voices to the far corners of larger and larger gatherings. The minister would be ecstatic that he could send his voice into peoples' homes across the land. God's word literally would be carried through the air.

So far, so good. But what about the accounting for the use of the gift of God? Would the many people who claim to speak for God be so enamored of the gadget and its power that they would forget its purpose?

My little parable has no point, at least not yet. We are still living the story so we don't know how it ends. We don't know whether the microphone is truly a gift of God to enhance our ability to carry his message or just another device appealing to human vanity and seducing us away from the true message.

Over all these years the message has stayed the same -- or at least it should have. It is the message of God's love and God's kingdom. Only the technologies for delivering it have really changed. These technologies -- microphones, cameras, radio waves, and satellites -- allow us to reach millions upon millions of communicants and parishioners and they will continue doing so during the years ahead.

We are using that equipment that is much more sophisticated, and our studio sets and production tools allow us to present the message in clearer, more vivid ways. We have an abundance of channels, as well, in our massive broadcast system.

But the idea of profit, which may never have entered the mind of the early preacher man, somehow seems to have become involved with the electronic ministry in recent years. We hear of the accumulation of dollars as often as we hear of the gathering in of converts. We hear of the building of earthly networks as often as we hear of God's kingdom. The cosmic message that warned we must account for the use of abuse of the magnificent communications instrument has more importance than ever before.

And so I ask, are we prepared to account for its use of abuse?

I know that this country includes some of the very best of responsible broadcasters. I know that they appreciate their influence -- and the responsibility it entails. They are conscious more and more of the power of the media they use in their ministry. These media can transform them as God's "point men," so to speak -- from simply the carriers of the word of God into false idols.

You have heard of how, in the distant past, emperors would behead the bearers of bad tidings. Even today we heap abuse upon those in the media who report bad news -- who merely bring us information that makes us uncomfortable or that portends unpleasant events.

It is possible that, instead of beheading the bearers of the good tidings of God's love or the bad tidings of God's wrath which abound in the electronic church, our audiences may embrace the messengers instead of the message. With their willingly given attention, these audiences may, in fact, turn an eloquent solicitor into a moneychanger in the temple.

The little old lady or gentleman who contributes a hard-earned or long-saved pittance expects it to further God's work, not to aggrandize the messenger. These millions of worshippers -- for that is what they are -- respond in faith to the pleas of their pastors. Their trust in the ministers of the airwaves is just as intense as that of those who sit in the pews of a church on Sunday morning. They count on their ministers to use their offerings to further the work of the church, to carry the same humble borne by that preacher man on the Western trail. They believe that their ministers, as bearers of God's message, will not abuse their trust, and they don't question those in whom they place their trust.

It seems to me that religious broadcasters, especially, would abhor such a stigma. It is good to know that, as a group, Christian broadcasters have come to insist on proper accounting procedures for funds raised over the air.

There is a parable in St. Matthew (13:24) that relates to the farmer who sowed good seed in his field. While he was sleeping, his enemy came and sowed weeds among the wheat, and when the field sprang forth with fruit, weeds also appeared. The servant, much distraught, came to his master and said, "Sir, didn't thou not sow good seed in thy field?" Some programming is packaged wheat but includes many weeds -- if it misleads people and takes advantage of their weaknesses or exploits their trust.

But this is only my opinion. As a former government official, I don't want to censor or control the content of programs, and under the law, it cannot be done.

This doesn't mean that those who program secular and religious material bear no responsibility for their programs. In a way, the absence of accountability to the government increases the programmer's accountability to some higher authority -- to the people and to God. The gift of the microphone includes a responsibility to use it for God's purposes, not just our own temporal satisfactions.

This responsibility to God -- and to our nationwide congregations, if you will -- also dictates the care with which the broadcaster should deal with social and political issues. It is one thing to exhort their viewers and listeners to be good citizens -- to raise their consciousness about the serious social and political issues of the day, but it is quite another matter to give the impression that certain political views or social standards are, indeed, scripturally inspired.

This use of the airwaves is perhaps more subtle than sowing the seeds of violence and pornography. There is just a small step from teaching the love of God to emphasizing the love of country and then extending that point to prescribing specific courses of involvement in current affairs.

The electronic church can lead audiences -- perhaps mistakenly -- into believing that strident claims of patriotism or extravagant defenses of certain notions of propriety are indeed the only answers to the great problems that beset our society. I am sad to admit that the questions we face in the world today do not always lend themselves to simple answers. It would be unfortunate if broadcast evangelists allowed themselves to become mere sloganeers for the proponents of some political positions on serious and complex national and international issues.

I am not suggesting that individuals or groups should not proclaim their religious or political beliefs or use the airwaves to do so. Indeed, as a former Commissioner with a long-standing interest in this subject, I have been telling broadcasters to do this very thing so that the public will be informed about the range of opinions on issues. What concerns me is the mingling of biblical teachings with political goals.

This subject is a sensitive one. I recognize the dilemma I am posing. After all, what is the point of God's teaching if it is not to teach us how to deal with the issues we face in the secular world? What is the point of God's messenger if he is not to show us how God's message relates to the world in which we live? Yet, I cannot help but feel uneasy when the answers to the serious issues of our time are glib and when isolated passages from the Bible are used to support a variety of inconsistent political positions. I fear that, in the effort to find God on our side of an issue, we may lose sight of the true word of God.

As, I said a few moments ago, the issues today have no easy solutions. Ministers as well as broadcasters have a challenging responsibility -- to teach us God's true message and to remind us that the message is relevant as much today as it was when Christ lived and the preacher man preached. All I ask is that they remember they are accountable for the message they carry and for how they carry it. The true message is what matters, not the medium or the messenger.

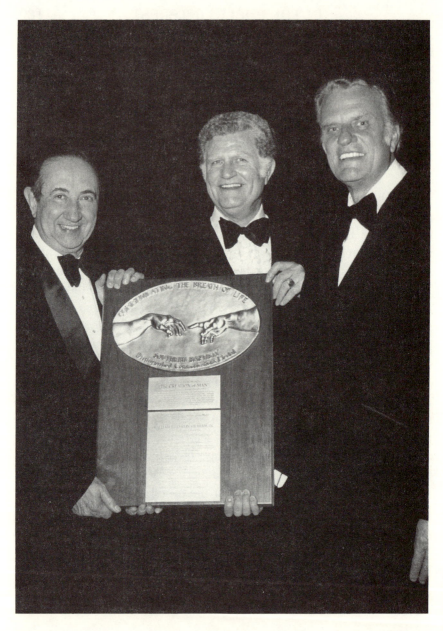

Accepting the "Communicating the Breathe of Life" Distinguished Communications Award from Jimmy R. Allen and the Reverend Billy Graham, Southern Baptist Radio and Television Convention, 1981.

14

REVOLUTION AND REGULATION

We are in the midst of a revolution. It's been bloodless so far, but the changes we are experiencing are as great in their own way as changes which often follow from wars and coups. The revolution I am referencing is technology -- electronics, computers, and communications. Old policies and structures based on old technology are giving way, and we must look for new ones. The Internet is simply the latest manifestation of a technological explosion. In this chapter I want to describe what happens when government regulation works, and how with vision and commitment, the FCC set the stage for the telecommunications revolution -- a revolution that is still underway in the 1990s and may never end.

A dramatic example of the need to adjust to technology comes from the early days of the telegraph in Europe. International telegraph messages were terminated at national boundaries, walked across the border, and retransmitted until they reached their final destinations. This is amusing, now, but we face the same kinds of problems today when we try to integrate electronic communications into new areas of our lives. For example, a major issue confronting the National Commission on Electronic Fund Transfers on which I represented the FCC concerns deployment of electronic fund terminals and the geographic area from which electronic deposits can be directly accepted by a financial institution.   In its February, 1977 Interim Report, the EFT Commission concluded that deposit taking is fundamental to a financial institution's relationship with its customers.   As a result, financial institutions should only be allowed to directly accept electronic deposits located within the or natural market areas where they are located.   Consumers, on the other hand, should have electronic access to their money anywhere there is a terminal capable of accessing the consumer's account. A problem arises when a consumer accesses his account to pay a bill in a store.   Should the corresponding electronic deposit to the merchant's account be made through a local financial institution before it can flow on to a financial institution in another part of the country?   The answer involves more than the technical capability of the computer and communications lines.   It will affect competition among financial institutions and both state and Federal banking policies.   When the full dimensions are considered, the solution is not always obvious or without controversy.

In the late 1970s, the FCC was in the throes of its second Computer Inquiry. This was an attempt to define the limits of the FCC's own jurisdiction in light of the merging of computer processing and communications processing technology.   The Inquiry was also an attempt to prescribe the rules by which regulated communications common carriers can participate in unregulated computer-related businesses.

To give you some understanding about why the FCC is involved in this question, consider how the communications industry and its regulation developed.

Modern telecommunications began when Samuel Morse invented the telegraph in the 1830's. By 1844, the government owned a telegraph line between Washington and Baltimore. However, the telegraph patents were privately held. These patents were offered to the government for $100,000, but Congress declined the purchase and, in 1846, offered the Washington/Baltimore circuit for sale or lease. With the exception of a brief period during the First World War, telecommunications in the United States has been a private sector business.

At first, several small companies offered telegraph service to the public. However, with mergers and failures, the telegraph business became concentrated in fewer and fewer companies, including the Western Union of Telegraph Companies. At the same time, lines were extended into the frontier, often in association with railroad expansion. In 1866, Congress passed the Post Road Act to give Federally franchised rights-of-way to encourage telegraph growth. This act also authorized the Postmaster to fix rates for government telegrams each year. Federal regulation of interstate electrical communications had begun.

In the same year, the first two submarine cables linking North America with Europe were laid by the Anglo-American Telegraph Company. By the late 1907s, there were more than 370,000 miles of submarine cable in the world. About 123,000 miles was telephone cable, and United States interests owned about 40 percent.

Between 1866 and 1876, Western Union enjoyed a period of sustained profitability and cams to dominate the telegraph industry. This lead to allegations of abuse such as free message service to public officials to influence legislation and favoritism to selected customers. Post office ownership was proposed as a remedy, but this idea was rejected. Instead, in 1887, Congress gave the Interstate Commerce Commission authority to require interconnection of telegraph lines.

After the telegraph, the most significant development in telecommunications came in 1876 when Alexander Graham Bell filed the first telephone patent --- three hours before Elisha Gray filed for a similar device. No one took this new gadget seriously at first. Indeed, Bell's backers offered to sell their patent to Western Union for $100,000, which was less than its development costs. Western Union declined. Within two years, however, Western Union realized its customers were beginning to use this new device. It bought the Gray patent, began its own telephone service, and found itself in a patent suit with Bell.

This suit was settled in 1879 with an agreement that laid the ground work for the present industry structure. Western Union kept the telegraph business, and Bell the telephone business. Bell also purchased a controlling interest in Western Union's manufacturing subsidiary, Western Electric, which is still a major Bell equipment supplier.

After the patent suit settlement, Bell placed about 266,000 telephones in operation. Then, in 1893, Bell's patent expired. A number of independent telephone companies entered the business to serve predominately small communities and rural areas. The number of telephones grew dramatically to over 3 million by 1907. The independents' lines couldn't be interconnected with Bell lines, however, and their attempts to finance their own long distance service failed. Between 1904 and 1914, 34 states passed laws requiring physical interconnection of lines.

As had happened earlier with regard to telegraph lines, many entities supported government ownership of telephone facilities. This movement ended in 1910 for all practical purposes when the Interstate Commerce Commission was given regulatory jurisdiction over interstate wire and radio common carriers under guidelines resembling those for the transportation carriers it also regulated. However, because the ICC was preoccupied with transportation matters, the Justice Department played a key role in defining Bell's growth and its relationship. with independent telephone companies. Bell was limited in its acquisition of competing telephone companies and competing telephone stations. It also pledged to connect independent telephone systems to its own toll system and thus became the unchallenged major provider of long distance service. In a later anti-trust suit, Bell agreed to limit its activity to communications equipment and services which could be offered under tariff.

In the 1970s, the telephone industry was composed of Bell and its 23 operating companies, which serve a little more than 41 percent of the continental United States and have more than 83 percent of the nation's telephones. Sixteen hundred independent telephone companies and several thousand rural telephone lines and systems served the rest. The total investment in America's telephone companies exceeded 119 billion dollars, about $768 for each of the nation's 155 million telephones.

Recognizing the problems of regulatory jurisdiction spread among the Interstate Commerce Commission, the Post Office Department, the State Department, and the Federal Radio Commission, Congress passed the Communications Act in 1934 to consolidate the regulation of all interstate communications matters under single regulatory authority, the FCC. With-seven commissioners and 2,150 employees in the 1970s, the FCC was responsible for regulating Bell with its almost one million employees and 3.9 billion dollar net income (in 1976), other interstate common carriers, several international carriers, several satellite carriers, more than 9,300 radio and television stations, about 10 million CB operators and a variety of other entities.

Until about the mid-1960's, the domestic communications industry was made up of a few companies which provided a limited number of homogeneous services. There was some competition between Bell and Western Union for private line service' that is, point-to-point dedicated communications lines which are reserved for specific customers, usually high volume users, on a full time basis. But, this market was a very small part of the Bell and

Western Union business. Also during this period, terminal equipment was fairly limited in-source and type.

In the mid-1960's, however, technology development outside the communications field radically expanded possible applications of the telephone network through use of specialized terminal equipment. These developments also created a demand for specialized private line capabilities which could not or might not be effectively provided over Bell and Western Union facilities.

The most significant development was the modern digital computer. The revolution started with the large, expensive computer capable of performing only one task at a time. Batch processing then developed to make use of idle time, but computer inputs and outputs still had to be hand carried to and from the computer site, and the user was not able to directly interact with the computer to make immediate corrections or data additions. Improvement came with time sharing which allowed the computer to handle more than one task at a time. Use of communications lines gave users access to the computer from other sites. Systems were developed using the ordinary dial-up telephone network and/or private lines to connect remote terminals with the central computer.

In addition, a need developed for computers at different places to talk to each other. But, the voice telephone channels were not perfect for this data communications need. Computers use "on-off" signals called bits to communicate. They operate at high speeds although their messages may last for only a few seconds. They require a high degree of accuracy in the transmission.

Voice channels designed to transmit sounds with a range of values are not naturally compatible with computer needs. Distortions due to transmission delays which are tolerable to the human ear are not tolerable to the computer. Even the 10 to 15 seconds needed to set up a call on the switched telephone network cause problems for computers for which complete message may last only a few seconds. Special interface devices called MODEMS or data sets were necessary to make telephone channels compatible with digital signals. Bell has also offered special "conditioning" for private lines to lower digital error rates. Both added to the cost of data communications and perhaps did not provide perfect solutions for the problem.

The computer revolution was accompanied by a revolution in electronics in general. The transistor, integrated circuits, and mini computers dramatically increased computer power while decreasing the size and cost of equipment needed to perform computer functions. This new technology had many potential applications within communications common carrier networks. It also meant that a large variety of terminals could be used to serve widely differing needs. Airline reservations, credit card verifications, electronic fund transfers, text editing, graph plotting, information retrieval, and computations are just some of the examples. The technology revolution which produced specialized requirements on the part of users also produced a large number of firms capable of supplying many of these needs.

At this point no one can predict where the revolution will end. Some think the pace of innovation is slowing down. The only things I am sure about are that more change is inevitable and the computer is inextricably linked with communications.

The changes we have already seen have caused the FCC to revise its thinking about communications and to review existing policies and practices. On one hand, the FCC should not prevent communications common carriers from using new technology. Such a restriction would make our communications system obsolete. It would also deny communications users the cost savings and system improvements new technology has made possible.

On the other hand, the FCC believed it should direct applications of the new technology to the benefit of users and consumers. The question was how to do this within the parameters of the Communications Act. Is it in the public interest to rely on a single terminal equipment supplier or is our traditional reliance on the marketplace more appropriate? What should be the appropriate boundary between regulated communications common carrier activities and unregulated data processing services? Are existing carrier services and facilities adequate to meet existing or future data communications needs? Should the bulk of the data communications market be left to only two competing suppliers, Bell and Western Union?

The FCC dealt with some of these questions in two lines of cases: one dealing with terminal equipment, the other with private line services. Its conclusion in both instances was that the public interest will best be served by full and fair competition in these two areas.

On the other hand, the FCC believed that basic telephone service, other than the provision of terminal equipment, should be opened to competition. Although technological distinctions between basic telephone service and private line services are sometimes fuzzy, the FCC was trying to develop a meaningful functional distinction.

The evolution of the FCC's policies regarding terminal equipment traced back to a court decision in 1956, the <u>Hush-A-Phone</u> case. The Hush-A-Phone was a cup-like device placed on a telephone hand set to funnel the speaker's voice into the telephone. Bell tariffs prohibited its customers from attaching any device to its lines, including the Hush-A-Phone. The court held this restriction was unlawful. In doing so, it established the principle that telephone subscribers have the right to use the telecommunications system in ways which are privately beneficial without being publicly detrimental. Tariffs restricting this right are considered unreasonable.

The FCC has applied this policy to all tariffs which provide a blanket prohibition against interconnection. However, the FCC has recognized that direct electrical connections of customer provided equipment could cause harm to the network. For this reason, it has adopted a program for registering protected circuits or complete terminal devices. Equipment meeting the technical requirements of the registration program can be marketed by anyone after it has been registered. Customers using this equipment no longer needed a telephone company to provide a protective device to attach this equipment to the telephone system. Terminal equipment provided by the telephone company would also have to be registered under the same standards which are applied to competitors.

The evolution of the FCC's policies regarding competing specialized common carriers traces back to a 1959 FCC decision authorizing businesses to build their own private microwave communications systems. Microwave technology developed after the Second World War have reduced the costs of building private systems, and the FCC saw no persuasive reason to restrict private use of this technology. Ten years later, the FCC authorized the first competing common carrier to use microwave for a new route between Chicago and St. Louis. This decision encouraged a number of additional applicants for specialized common carrier service. In 1970, the FCC initiated an overall policy and rule-making proceeding to study the general question of common carrier competition. It concluded that increased competition for specialized services would stimulate technology and service innovation and would give data users needed flexibility. As a result, the FCC decided not to restrict new entry into the specialized common carrier business. This rationale was applied to "value-added" carriers which provide an additional service, such as packet switching, to lines leased from other common carriers.

Finally, in July, 1976, the FCC made what may become the most significant change in private line communications policy with the adoption of a policy favoring the unlimited resale and sharing of common carrier private line facilities and services. Resale is the subscription to communications services and facilities by one entity which then offers those services and facilities to the public (with or without "adding value") for profit. Sharing is a non-profit arrangement in which several users collectively use and share the cost for communications services and facilities offered by a carrier. Entities which resell communications services would be regulated as common carriers. Sharing arrangements which do not constitute the offering of services for a profit would not be subject to that regulation.

These actions led to a two-tiered interstate telecommunications industry structure. The first tier consisted of carriers which offer basic communications channels and switching services at the "retail" level to the public and at the "wholesale" level to other common carriers and resale carriers. The second tier was made up of entities which lease the preponderance of their communications plant from the first tier carrier and then resell that plant to the public to serve specialized sub-markets. Rather than harm the first tier carriers such as Bell and the independent telephone companies, the FCC actions expanded resale and sharing to stimulate the demand for communications services while offering the user greater flexibility.

One of the most difficult tasks the FCC has dealt with has been the delineation of those activities which are data processing, and thus beyond its jurisdiction. In 1971, the FCC decided that communications common carriers subject to its jurisdiction may not provide data processing through a separate corporate subsidiary. It was concerned about the allocation of common costs between data processing and communications services if both were provided by a carrier. Unduly complicated costs allocations would frustrate the FCC's regulation of common carrier rates. Thus, common carriers currently are foreclosed from directly offering predominantly data processing services, They are also foreclosed from directly offering terminal devices which only or primarily perform data processing functions.

This decision seemed to establish a meaningful distinction for the FCC's purposes. But, the computer and electronics revolution moved in directions not anticipated by the FCC. The phenomenon of the distributed computer network has blurred the communications and data processing distinction even more than it was in the early 1970s. Now new computers and terminal devices can perform both data processing and communications control functions within the network and at the terminal.

As you can see, competition is an important part of the FCC's concern. The FCC looks to competition in some areas to increase innovation, provide diversity, and decrease costs to the consumer. The FCC has made some controversial decisions which may initially appear inconsistent with the goal of low cost service to some segments of the using public. However, according to the Communications Act, common carrier rates must be just and reasonable. One way to evaluate the rates is to look at their cost justifications. The FCC tries to determine whether particular costs should be included in the carrier's revenue requirements and whether those costs are properly allocated to the appropriate service. This has never been an easy task. With the growth in communications common carrier use and the increased diversity in services, the task has become more difficult, both for the FCC and for the carriers. The FCC was particularly concerned about hidden cross-subsidies between services. Without a public policy reason to the contrary, the FCC in my time did not believe that users of one service should subsidize users of another. It also did not believe that computers can fairly compete with improperly subsidized services.

In the long-run these decisions may make more meaningful

competition possible. Changes are inevitable. We must all hope that these changes will bring us benefits. Making this happen is the challenge presented to the FCC and to each of us by the technology revolution.

"Bob, what's all this crap about you wanting to resign?"   With
President Lyndon Baines Johnson, the White House, 1967.

"Congratulations on a job well done!" With President Ronald
Reagan, the White House, 1981.

15

LOYALTIES

I am often asked why partisan loyalty outweighs technical knowledge of broadcasting in commission appointments. When President Eisenhower first nominated me, one of the principal criticisms -- aside from my friendship with Joe McCarthy -- was my lack of broadcasting expertise. It was a valid objection, one that was raised in a <u>Washington Post</u> editorial. On the other hand, laymen committed to serving the public are less likely than experts from the communications industry to become captives of their clients.

It took me two or three years to feel comfortable in dealing with the kinds of problems our engineers advised us on. The need for this long training period led me to believe that an FCC Commissioner should be appointed for only one term but of long duration, perhaps fifteen years, like the Comptroller General of the United States. My experience on the Hill and my high regard for the nonpartisan work of the official who headed the General Accounting Office convinced me that this kind of policy change would strengthen the FCC -- and perhaps other regulatory agencies -- and lift it above the frequent charges of partisan and business favoritism.

I enjoyed my associations with my fellow Commissioners

whatever our political or ideological differences; several of them have been close friends and golfing partners since we left the agency. I liked the give and take of our exchange of views -- - bargaining over the rate of return of AT&T. For example, before the inhibiting effect of the opening of our meetings to the public; that reform, which sprang from Watergate, was another mixed blessing. Our earlier deliberations were collegial. In later years the power of the Chairman, who determines the agenda of the sessions, tightened procedures and sometimes made our sessions seem like a one-man show.

***

I never longed to be Chairman myself, except briefly just before my retirement. Which brings me to my reappointments in 1967, 1974, and 1981.

My renomination by Lyndon Johnson in 1967 followed a tortuous pas de deux between me and the President. My term was due to expire June 30, and despite assurances from my friends and the trade press that my reappointment was assured, I was nervous. If they were wrong I needed a job. So, when a couple of Illinois friends, Bill Putnam and Red Quinlan, took me to lunch and asked me if I would be interested in becoming president of a new all-channel trade association, I asked them to draw up a proposal. I then told Chairman Hyde to alert the White House to expect my letter of resignation. He tried to talk me out of the idea but I said no.

The trade association offer looked good, and I asked my legal associate to help me draw up a contract. Chairman Hyde again asked me to reconsider, saying that he was authorized to speak for the President. When I again declined, he asked me to make the effective date of my resignation at the pleasure of the President. A few days later, Putnam and Quinlan returned the contract, which they had signed, and gave me thirty days to decide. I immediately sent a letter to the President tendering my resignation at his pleasure.

On July 5, the Commission's first meeting day after these maneuvers, I advised my colleagues of my resignation and said I couldn't vote on matters that might conflict with my prospective new job. That afternoon a phone call from the White House told me the President wanted to see me and that I shouldn't make any commitments until after I had talked with him.

We tentatively scheduled a meeting for 11:30 A.M. July 11, and I went into semi-seclusion until then. Meantime the story of my imminent resignation leaked out and I was besieged by reporters. I talked freely and a flood of publicity resulted, which apparently irked White House officials, and Hyde asked me to make no further comment.

On Monday, July 10, Joe Califano called me from the White House and said my appointment would be at 6:00 P.M. the next day. I spent that day in seclusion and took no phone calls, except one from Califano about 3:00 P.M. changing the meeting to 5:45 P.M. and then one about 4:45 P.M. from the President's special assistant, Marvin Watson, saying that it would be put off for several days. He was obviously annoyed by press questions about my meeting with LBJ and indicated he (Watson) wanted to have an off-the-record talk with me.

I did a lot of soul searching the next few days. It annoyed me that I couldn't get out of the government without White House approval, but I was determined not to stay unless the President himself asked me to. While I was stewing, some people were mounting a campaign to keep me on the Commission, partly out of friendship but mainly because they needed my vote on matters where the balance was in doubt. H.L. Hunt and several influential members of Congress urged me to stay on the FCC.

I felt the vise getting tighter and tighter. My deadline for signing the contract was August 2, and I couldn't ethically sign it until I was out of government. I made up my mind that I would call the White House and urge acceptance of my resignation; otherwise I would be compelled to write another letter setting a specific date. Then one evening Senator Dirksen phoned me at home urging me to reconsider leaving the Commission. I told him my dilemma and said it would require the President's personal intervention to prevent my leaving. He then told me I would get a call from Marvin Watson and urged me to discuss the matter with him.

As Dirksen said, Watson suddenly summoned me to the White House. But instead of asking me to sit down to talk, he immediately ushered me into the Oval Office, where a smiling President said, "How are you, Bob?"

"I think I'm about to faint," I replied.

Then, "What's this crap about you going to resign?"

"Mr. President, I am at your disposal," I said.

"OK; that's taken care of," he told me. "Now, I would like to show you my dogs."

The next hour and a half astonishes me still. As if he had all the time in the world, the President took me by the shoulder and walked me to the kennels, where there were four beagles and a beautiful white collie. He let them loose and they ran all over the place, much to his enjoyment. As we walked around the grounds, he talked constantly, occasionally nudging me in the ribs with his elbow as he rambled on. I said "Yes, Mr. President" or "No, Mr. President" time after time to his queries. One question I had to handle delicately. When he asked what I thought of our newest Commissioner, Nicholas Johnson, I indicated that he was obviously very bright and attributed the trouble he gave Chairman

Hyde to his youth. LBJ's response suggested that he was sorry he had appointed him.

Returning to business, the President said our friend Styles Bridges would rise from his grave if I were not reappointed to the Commission. Rosel Hyde and I, he said, were his real friends on the FCC; he loved us and he knew we loved him. The government needed "good young men" -- though I was nearly as old as he was. He intimated that even though I was a Republican, I might succeed Hyde as Chairman. Or if I should become interested in some other Federal position, he was always looking for Republican judges. I didn't tell him I wasn't a lawyer.

Back in his office, the President showed me some paintings, by a friend of his, and gleefully told me he had bought ten of them for $2,000 apiece and was now selling them for $5,000 each to other friends. He autographed two photos for me and arranged to send a small bronze bust of himself to my wife. (I'm afraid the gift to Rex could be seen on many mantels in and out of Washington.)

As we parted, LBJ brought up the name of Sol Taishoff, the publisher of Broadcasting magazine, and spoke warmly about their friendship over the years. On this note, I floated out into the real world. My Commander-in-Chief needed me, and I simply couldn't turn him down. My nomination for another seven-year term went promptly to the Senate. After a brief hearing before the Commerce Committee, I was unanimously confirmed.

***

My last two appointments came more easily. In 1974, although two students of the appointments process say there was not unanimity in Nixon's White House, Vice President Jerry Ford lent his support. And with the President under siege following Watergate, it was no time for him to offend my friends in Congress. I had evidently been considered the year before for an appointment as Chairman of the Commission. At least my old friend from Capitol Hill days, Mel Laird, serving as Nixon's domestic affairs adviser, penned in a postscript to me: "If the Chairmanship is offered -- don't decline."

In January 1981, after Ronald Reagan's election to the presidency, I announced my intention to retire on June 30. Since the Chairman, Charles Ferris, wasn't acceptable to the new Administration, I assumed that I would be named interim Chairman for the remaining few months of my term. I wanted the Chairmanship simply to have it on my record. But, Reagan's transition team had ideas I didn't know about, and while I, as senior Commissioner, assumed the chair in an acting capacity, I waited for some time for an expected letter from the President naming me to the position until Ferris's successor came on board. As Broadcast magazine reported in February, I joked about my disappointment at not hearing anything from the White House: "Even if it said 'Merry Christmas,' just so long as it was signed by the President."

I learned through an article in Broadcast magazine that the President planned to appoint an interim chairman until he could qualify his own people. Again, as the ranking Republican, I hoped that he would choose me. I was surprised, however, to learn that my colleague Abbott Washburn was also interested in the position. Abbott and I were always good friends and I knew this wasn't a matter of personal rivalry. In fact, he came to me and said the interim chairmanship wasn't worth fighting about. So we decided then and there to let the process take care of itself and let the President pick whomever he wanted.

I knew that there was gossip against me, mainly the fact that I was on friendly terms with Charlie Ferris. many of the broadcasters simply did not like him, even though he was a hard working, honest, and competent chairman. I believed that he made substantial contributions during his tenure. perhaps the real problem was personal -- Ferris was not as accessible as many people would have liked. Broadcasters found it difficult to meet with him. But while I often differed with him on major issues, we had a warm personal relationship.

The broadcaster's anger was further stoked by Ferris' desire to remain on the Commission payroll after resigning as chairman. Immediately after the Inauguration, there was a complication concerning Ferris' pension. It turned out that in order to qualify for a minimum pension for twenty years of government service, Charlie would have to stay on the roll until May 10, 1981. So, an arrangement was worked out that allowed Ferris to stay until that date, but in effect he would not participate in the work of the Commission. So, Charlie explained all of this, and I understood. But, the broadcasters didn't like this, and were vocal in their opposition, which didn't help my cause any.

The first meeting after the Inauguration, I took the chair and announced that, as was the custom of the FCC over the years, the ranking Commissioner would act in the absence of the Chairman. I asked if their was any objection, and hearing none, I became Acting Chairman. Yet, it was awkward trying to run the Commission without Presidential authority. But I soon received a phone call from the White House, informing me that the President had signed an order making me Acting Chairman. I even received a letter from the President thanking me for filling-in, without suggesting an appointment to be the permanent chairman.

We went along on that basis until Charlie's time was up. Then, much to my delight, the President officially made me the chairman. It turned out that this lasted for only three or four weeks, but I held the position until Mark Fowler was confirmed.

***

I have passed over several of my special interests in my long career on the FCC. My main accomplishment was the promotion of UHF television broadcasting, but I was also a principal champion of FM radio broadcasting. I was an early advocate of subscription television. An article I wrote for Look magazine in March 1956 carried the message, "Let's give the public a chance at paid TV." The St. Louis Post-Dispatch, a newspaper that had bitterly opposed my appointment to the FCC, warmly applauded my stand on this issue.

Serving on the Commission gave me a "bully pulpit" for preaching to broadcasters in my frequent appearances before their conventions. Some of them probably grew weary of hearing "Lee's Ten Commandments":

1. Know thy community as thyself.
2. Serve thy community as it deserves.
3 Keep faith with the Commission and the FCC will place its faith in thee.
4. Practice the use of discretion, judgment, and good taste.
5. Foul not the airways.
6. Place not your faith in ratings -- thou are a better judge.
7. Turn away from payola.
8. Remember the sanctity of the fairness doctrine.
9. Minimize contests and promotions -- they reflect thy character.
10. Remember to keep holy the National Association of Broadcasters codes.

When I retired on June 30, 1981, I was the dean of all Federal Commissioners. In my almost 28 years on the FCC, I had served with 28 of the 55 Commissioners appointed to the agency since the passage of the Communications Act of 1934. With only two possible exceptions, I considered them good and honorable men.

Besides providing me with many friends and wonderful memories, the years since my purchase of an elementary book on electricity in 1953 had taught me enough about the communications industry that I was looking forward to an exciting new career: helping the creation of direct broadcasting to the home by means of a geo-stationary satellite.

Bob Lee, with his wife, Rose Ann Bente Lee, and former FCC Commissioner Benjamin Hooks, National Association of Broadcasters Salute to Robert E. Lee, 1977. Note the portrait of the new "General Lee."

16

RETIREMENT

I surely didn't slow down when I retired, but the backdrop changed. Instead of the daily grind of the FCC, I was free to set my own schedule, which meant it was even harder to refuse a request. But I was able to test new waters, and start fresh on new projects of interest.

I was supported by the friendships of a lifetime, and by the appreciation of the telecommunications community. My retirement from the Commission brought me a flood of congratulatory letters on my career. That was to be expected, of course. Anyone leaving a job he has held for twenty-eight years is entitled to some sort of recognition, even from the grumpy guy who was always humming what sounded like "I'll be glad when you're dead, you rascal, you!"

What wasn't expected was the warmth and sentiment of so many of the obligatory letters. I especially liked Sol Taishoff's mixture of insult and flattery: "You're too old and ugly to be a glamour boy and too profane to be a Saint, but in the hearts of your countrymen -- Irish, Jewish, Catholics, or Arab -- your name is among the top as a decent, warm, God-fearing human being."

Former Chairman Dean Burch welcomed me "to the world of the

once weres, where dinner invitations decline, reservations are hard to make, phone calls don't get returned, and no one concedes three-foot putts."

Another former Chairman, Newton Minnow, credited me with giving him the phrase that made him famous to highbrows, infamous to the broadcasting trade. Coming to the FCC "young, green and inexperienced," he wrote, "I asked you for your advice. You told me I should call television a 'vast wasteland.' I have been in trouble ever since. After I made the speech, you told me that I misunderstood -- that you meant 'half-vast.'" If President Reagan didn't make me ambassador to Ireland -- a job I would really have liked -- Minnow suggested, "How about Iran?" This, remember, was when Ayatollah Khomeini was our premier bete noire.

Other colleagues joked about my jokes; although I complained about broadcasters who allowed dirty jokes and sleazy innuendoes on the air, I was said to have the biggest collection of off-color stories in Washington. Frederick Ford reminded me of the funny stories I told when introducing Danny Thomas -- "Poor Danny, he was anti-climactic." And William Henry remembered my saying how shocked my father was when he heard I had become a Republican. "It can't be true," he told his friends. "I saw Bob at Mass just last Sunday!"

My colleagues' references to my fondness of funny stories -- especially Irish ones -- remind me of one of the great satisfactions of my career on the Commission. I love to make people laugh. And I like to laugh with them. Looking through the pictures in my scrapbooks, I see myself laughing as heartily as my audience. I don't know how many times I opened a speech with a favorite joke about a caddie and a priest, but it always seemed as fresh and funny to me as when I first heard it. Humor, I found, not only eased tension when I broached unpopular ideas to an unfriendly gathering of broadcasters but promoted understanding and acceptance of my ideas.

***

I suppose I must like sometimes to be the center of attention, to show off what talents I possess. At a recent family dinner party in Chicago my ninety-one year-old brother reminded me of an incident I had forgotten about my youth in Prohibition days. In our Irish neighborhood there were a number of basement "blind pigs" or speakeasies where the right password would open the door. One of these was Matt Schulein's place -- he later became a famous magician -- where I picked up a little change on Saturday nights singing and doing a softshoe dance routine. One night my older brother came into the place and caught me in my act. He complained to Matt and told him, "Get that kid out of here." Matt replied, "We'll throw you out first."

I made hundreds of speeches when I was on the FCC on a wide array of subjects pertaining to broadcasting. They took me all over the country and, instead of honoraria, which I couldn't accept, brought me a lot of titles and certificates: honorary membership in the Order of the Alaskan Sourdough, a colonelcy in the Confederate Air Force, Wyoming Bronc Buster, honorary citizenship of Texas and of Louisville, Kentucky, membership in the Institute of Electrical and Electronic Engineers, and so on.

Besides the trivial and perfunctory certificates, welcome as they were as mementos of interesting occasions, I received several honors I prized highly. Fordham University's Department of Communication Arts presented me with a citation of excellence, especially for my advocacy of educational television, and I received a similar citation from Indiana University's Department of Radio and Television.

***

My Catholic faith brought many of my speech invitations and provided the occasion for recognition of my work on the Commission. In 1968, for example, I received the Award of Merit of the Catholic Apostolate of Mass Media for my "commitment to the expanded use of radio and television as instruments of entertainment, enlightenment and education." And I'm proud to remember that Baptists honored me too. In 1981, the year of my retirement from the FCC, -I received the Distinguished Communicators Award from the Baptist Radio and Television Commission at their annual Abe Lincoln Awards to Distinguished Broadcasters ceremony. I took that occasion in Dallas to vent my strong feelings about preachers who broadcast for profit and mingle "biblical teachings with political goals."

Three Catholic universities -- St. John's, Notre Dame, and St. Bonaventure -- added me to their alumni rolls in their commencement ceremonies. St. John's and Notre Dame honored my public service by awarding the degree of Doctor of Law. St. Bonaventure awarded me an honorary degree as Doctor of Science. An honorary doctorate from Notre Dame -- where I had longed to go to college years before but could not afford to -- filled me with pride. Father Theodore Hesburgh, when he was president of the university, and Father Edmund "Ned" Joyce, his chief assistant and the school's executive vice president, welcomed my idea of establishing a telecommunications institute in the university. But when we estimated the endowment needed for the institute, we had to abandon the ambitious scheme.

My experience on the FCC and my continuing interest in broadcasting also led a Washington law firm -- Fletcher, Heald & Hildreth -- to offer me a position as their telecommunications consultant.

Also, the Voice of America asked me to help launch the Radio Marti broadcasts to Castro's Cuba. In my view, these broadcasts have been very helpful in giving the Cuban people vital information that will one day lead to the restoration of democracy.

Accepting an honorary "Doctor of Law" degree from President Theodore Hesburgh, University of Notre Dame, South Bend, Indiana, 1978.

17

DIRECT SATELLITE BROADCASTING

An idea I haven't abandoned, and one which has kept me employed since my retirement from the FCC, is DBS -- direct broadcasting by satellite. I became intensely interested in DBS in 1973, giving speeches on it and writing a series of articles that were published in Television/Radio Age in March and April of that year. Until the advent of satellites, high quality telephone, record and radio broadcasting were available only within the United States, including adjacent areas of Canada and within Europe and Japan. World coverage of TV news, however, was still no quicker than the old Fox Movietone features provided in theaters in the 1930's. Even in the developed countries, people could see firsthand what was going on around the world only as quickly as film clips could be flown to the TV networks. The rest of the world remained in virtual isolation.

In an age of CNN and MTV, where satellite broadcasting unites our global village, it's difficult to remember just how satellites changed our world-view. Satellite technology introduced a whole new concept in international communications, for the satellite enables many countries, or even areas within countries, to communicate directly with each other and to relay all forms of communications at the same time -- telephone, television, record, data, and facsimile services. Now, we take it for granted that someone in the bush outside Anchorage can speak via satellite with someone in the outback of Australia. Video pictures can bounce off the satellite from Zimbabwe to Warsaw. Faxs can be sent from Singapore to Santiago. This instant access has made our world a neighborhood -- and we are sometimes more familiar with events in Jakarta or St. Petersburg than on our own block.

Even back in 1969, the miracle of TV transmission via satellite made it possible for one out of every four people on earth to see Neil Armstrong take man's first step on the moon. This was the most widely shared moment in history and probably demonstrated for the first time the magnitude of the impact that satellite technology would have on the future.

Shortly before I left the Commission in June 1981, Stanley S. Hubbard, a broadcaster from St. Paul, Minnesota, spoke to me about joining his organization as a consultant. I had already been offered a board membership at COMSAT, the government's telecommunication agency, but Hubbard's offer was renewed soon after I retired. It was more attractive to me because I saw the startling potential of DBS -- in my mind it was the next frontier, the next step in technology. I wanted to be on the cutting-edge of telecommunications, so I eagerly accepted board membership with Hubbard Communications. Since my appointment was backdated to the day after I left the government, I like to brag that I have never been unemployed a single day since I was in the sixth grade as a schoolboy.

In the broadcasting industry, the Hubbard family is legendary. Stanley E. Hubbard, the founder of the Hubbard broadcasting empire, consisting of some seven television stations, radio stations, and associated enterprises, was well-known for vision and innovation. He was a pioneer who shaped and molded American telecommunications. For example, Stanley E. Hubbard was the first person to operate a radio station supported by commercial advertising. He was the first to transmit live dance music by putting a transmitter in a dance hall and broadcasting a live band. He undertook the first remote broadcast, covering a golf tournament. He was one of the first to analyze weather using doppler radar. Hubbard saw that black-and-white broadcasting was too unrealistic, and so he was the first to buy a color camera and the first to broadcast all-color. He owned the first NBC affiliate. His communications empire was even responsible for building the first satellite truck -- known as a "GTAC Truck" (Garbage Truck Air Conditioning).

Stanley E. was an exciting, far-sighted, and truly great man -- the product of an American Dream that matched courage with conviction.

The latest project of Hubbard Communications, of which Stanley S. was now in charge following his father's death, concerned the launching of a geo-stationary satellite capable of sending a signal directly into people's homes rather than depending on any physical interconnection, as with the cable industry. The family had already spent millions of dollars in research and engineering and hopes to launch the satellite early in 1994. While the concept is new in the United States, Japan, Germany, and the United Kingdom have already proved that it is workable.

My job was to counsel the company on how best to make this new technology financially viable for its backers and for the American people. DBS became my passion, and whenever I wondered about my remaining years, I vowed that I would do everything possible to get that satellite launched. As I write this, the satellite isn't up yet. But it is now only a matter of time. [Collaborator's Note: a DBS satellite was successfully launched in June 17, 1994, after Mr. Lee's death.] After the satellite launch, it will probably take seven or eight years before the enormous undertaking becomes profitable for its backers. As I told a newspaper interviewer, I may be one of the richest people in the graveyard when the returns finally begin to flow. The reason for the delayed payoff is that advertisers are unlikely to buy broadcast time until they know that there are enough sets capable of receiving the signal.

The problem is much like the one I described earlier facing the development of UHF broadcasting. The FCC tried every means it could think of to encourage the marketplace to convert existing television sets so that they could receive both VHF and UHF signals, but we finally had to persuade the Congress to use its power to regulate interstate commerce to force their manufacture. It then took about two years for the industry to develop the techniques and make the necessary machine tools to produce the instrument; it took about seven years more for enough old receiving sets to be replaced by the new to enable UHF stations to compete effectively with their VHF counterparts. We now need the Congress to make that requirement -- to stipulate that television manufacturers must include conversion technology for satellite reception with each new model. This will increase consumer choice and escalate the acceptance of DBS.

Could the FCC resort to the same all-channel law to force the development of a new mechanism capable of receiving the DBS signals? In my analysis of this complex problem, I concluded that the Commission has the legal authority, after a rule-making, to require that all sets manufactured for sale in interstate commerce be capable of receiving all "broadcast" signals.

Many problems await solution. One of the biggest is to find programming attractive enough to viewers to lead them to buy a new television set. We have suggested to interest groups that we might offer free advertising time in return for their helping to promote conversion to a set capable of receiving the DBS signal. We are also thinking of picking up the French satellite signal and rebroadcasting it in the United States, of providing a channel for children's programming, and perhaps of cooperating with the United States Information Agency in broadcasting to Cuba or elsewhere.

Obviously the problem of developing and promoting DBS is a formidable one, but I am convinced that we are capable of meeting the challenge and that the rewards for investors and for the American viewing audience will be worth the effort. If it does what we expect it to, it will revolutionize television. It will provide a direct line to the home and no big dish will clutter up the yard. Rather, a small antenna in the window will do the trick, and only people with the correct receiving sets will be able to pick up the broadcasting signal.

Commencement Address, St. Bonaventure, Olean, New York, 1983. Mr. Lee received an honorary degree signifying "Doctor of Science".

Investiture as a Knight of Malta, Sovereign Military Order of
Malta, Federal Association, United States, 1983.

A legal consultation: Bob Lee with the late Chief Justice of the Supreme Court, Warren Burger, and former Federal Circuit Judge, U.S. Court of Appeals (District of Columbia Circuit), Robert Bork, Annual Thomas More Society Gala, Washington, D.C., 1988.

18

IRELAND -- FOREVER HOME

There are passings that accompany life. My first wife, Rex, died in 1972 after a long siege fighting cancer. She was in and out of hospitals for seven or eight years, and I had become resigned to the certainty of her leaving me. But even her release from pain hardly lessened my grief.

My present wife, Rose, the widow of Raymond H. Bente, is one of the most remarkable persons I have ever known. Rose was born near Fulda in Germany, the youngest of twelve children. She escaped the wartime trials of her native country by emigrating to the United States. She made the long journey and lived with a brother in Hyattsville, Maryland, a suburb of Washington, D.C. Through hard work and masterful management abilities, she became well-known in Washington as the owner of chain of successful fabrics stores.

Rose claims it took six months for me to risk accepting a dinner invitation at her friend's house on the Patuxent River in Maryland to make her acquaintance! Even when I finally came to dinner, I brought a male friend along.

I knew right away that I had met the woman I wanted to marry. And Rose says that she was ready to marry me the next day. So my courtship was blessedly short and we were soon married. Now, nearly twenty years later, I know it was one of the wisest and happiest choices I have ever made.

***

Nearly every year my wife, Rose Anne, and I travel to Ireland, the birthplace of my parents. They were born in Galway County, on Ireland's west coast, and Galway town has come to seem like a familiar second home to me.

My first trip to Ireland, though, in 1952, didn't take me there. It was only a short trip to Dublin with a couple of Republican congressmen. They had joined my inspection team in London, where we had conducted an investigation for the House Appropriations Committee. One of them made arrangements with the U.S. ambassador to Ireland to visit him. I recall with amusement how embarrassed the young ambassador was when his wife, evidently a Democrat, gushed on about her admiration for Adlai Stevenson and how hard it was to decide between him and Eisenhower for President. Her red-faced husband quickly changed the subject.

It was not until twenty-one years later that I visited the ancestral home in Galway County. On my way back from an international telecommunications conference in Geneva, I flew into Shannon Airport and met my two sons there. I remember that they were grinning and hiding behind newspapers when I walked into the lounge.

"If you ever go across the sea to Ireland..." At home on the "ol' sod" with son Michael near Galway Bay, 1973.

"At the closing of the day..." In front of Mr. Day's, a restaurant and bar known for its fine food and hospitality, with the owner, son Robert.

"So, Dad, what's up today?" Mr. Lee and sons Michael and Robert.

Family reunion with brother Edward and sister Margaret, standing in back, and sisters Mildred (Mary Cecelia) and Elanore, seated left to right, with brother Bob, Chicago, 1985.

We rented a car and drove to Galway town. My cousin Ann Lee had a pub there. Her father -- my uncle -- had been a policeman in Chicago and then returned to Ireland, where he became a successful businessman.   Ann had a typically Irish sense of humor. If a customer asked her for a newspaper, she would ask, "Would you like today's or yesterday's?" If he said "Today's," she'd tell him, "Well, you'll have to come back tomorrow."

I learned a lot of family history on that trip. One of my cousins, a priest, also named Robert E. Lee, took me to his father, a schoolteacher, who spent two or three hours relating local and family lore into my tape recorder. Father Lee's brother showed me around Galway College, where he was the principal executive officer and where my cousin Nell was a chemistry professor.

I saw Nell again and many others of my kinfolk on a trip Rose and I made in 1991. I asked Father Lee to gather as many as he could for a dinner at a local hotel. Fifty-five showed up, all adults; I suppose if all their progeny had come we could have filled an auditorium. The priest played his violin and we had a great time. The next year, 1992, we returned to find more than 80 family members and friends at an encore party.

These family gatherings mean a lot to me. If I chartered an airliner and transported all of my own family to Galway on one of those annual expeditions, we could really make the town bulge. My three children -- Patricia, Robert, and Michael -- have given me fifteen grandchildren.   Pat and her engineer husband -- a graduate of Virginia Military Institute whose army career took them all over the world -- have seven children. They now live in Yorktown, Virginia, where he became York County's director of public works after retiring from the military. Bobby, who owns three restaurants in the Washington, D.C. area, and two in Florida, is the father of seven children. And Mike, a very successful executive vice-president of a company owning a chain of hotels, has three children. So far, as of June, 1995, I have nineteen great-grandchildren. It's quite a family and I'm proud of them.

In 1991, we had a grand family reunion in Chicago on St. Patrick's Day. All of my sisters and my brother were still alive. Even in his nineties, Edward is still sharp and vibrant. He had a successful career as a certified public accountant. Margaret, the oldest sister, worked for a telephone company before her marriage; her husband has now died. Mildred, in her eighties, joined a convent when sixteen, and has had a marvelous career teaching and administering in parochial schools; she doesn't look a day over fifty. The baby of the family, Elanore, seventy-six, sharply corrected my introduction of her when I said she was two years older than that.

It was good to be together again in our old home city. The Chicago River was dyed green for the day and green banners decked the buildings. Rose and I sat in the reviewing stand and watched the Irish politicians parade by. Irish policemen, like my father in my boyhood, lined the streets. I even heard familiar words drifting on the wind, the strains of "Galway Bay."

####

APPENDIX 1

THE SPEECHES OF ROBERT E. LEE

[Collaborator's Note: Mr. Lee was a highly regarded speaker. As a Commissioner at the FCC, Mr. Lee spoke almost on a daily basis. Even in his years of retirement, Bob often was called upon to "find the words" to make an occasion memorable. After sifting through hundreds of speeches, I decided to include this representative sample. My guiding principle was their relevance for current telecommunications policy and/or their timeless messages. The reader may find the first, a radio broadcast from 1954, extremely interesting because of its optimistic declaration of Mr. Lee's religious faith and his faith in man. These values, apparent so early in his career, were formative in developing the views later expressed at the FCC. The last presentation in this section is a set of notes for a speech given after leaving the FCC. In that speech Mr. Lee reminds his audience of the important role of the FCC, a message that is most topical in the mid-1990s, when telecommunications policy and the future of the FCC are passionate, consuming, and vital issues. The rest of the speeches bracketed by this pair concern the broadcasting industry and its need for wise self-regulation. A commencement speech is also included, illustrating Mr. Lee's continued optimism in the future as people learn to expand their horizons.]

235

"Faith in our Times"
Remarks by Robert E. Lee
Radio Address
National Council of Catholic Men
in cooperation with the
Mutual Broadcasting System
March 30, 1954

It has been said that man's most critical age is the one in which he happens to be currently living. Does anyone recall when we were not living in an age of crisis? Will a statesman ever proclaim that there is peace and tranquility in the world and that disaster of one form or another is not "Imminent"? How valid is the faith of these prophets of doom? If men of all nations publicly professed their faith in the wisdom and guidance of a Supreme Being perhaps the world might come closer to the tranquility that has thus far eluded us.

I remember seeing sometime ago a picture post card put out by Boys Town, Nebraska. It showed two ragged youngsters, the older of whom carried the younger on his shoulders. The caption read. "He's not heavy, he's my brother." This is, indeed, a practical expression of faith in the beautiful example that a little child shall lead them. Faith, in a manner of speaking, is brotherhood and brotherhood is faith in your fellow man that he too will respond to reason and good will.

One of the most striking things about our life is that it does not carry with it the answers to its own questions. We can find out for ourselves to get from others a knowledge of how to make a living and of how to get along on a day to day basis with our fellow men. But there are many questions out beyond that area which cry for an answer and for which no adequate answer is provided by the data that life gives.

What is life? Where does it come from? What is it for? That is to say, beyond the enjoyment of each successive day, beyond the abundant disappointments and frustrations, what is the reason of our having life? Why does life end so soon? What is beyond it? What do the actions of each day in this life contribute to the happiness or unhappiness of a possible life beyond this sphere? These are the questions that life itself gives no answer to. And yet there must be answers. Else why should we have the insistent urge to ask the questions.

To me, my faith means the answers to these questions. St. Paul says that faith is "the evidence of things unseen." The unseen realities of the spiritual and everlasting world are made real to me by my faith revealed by God and transmitted by his Church.

Faith in our times should be positive and not negative. Faith should take the form of positive expression that this is indeed God's country, where freedom has reached new heights and woe betide those who would take it from us. Yes, we have our faults. We may have made mistakes we bitterly regret, but never mistakes of the heart, and Faith has sustained us.

When I look at this wonderful country and the God-fearing people that comprise its membership, I have no fear for the future. We have our problems. We are facing an ideological struggle with a foreign, godless, atheistic communism that has found too many supporters amongst our ranks and too many dupes who plead cause in full ignorance of what they do. The godless and the atheistic will fall in the future as they have always fallen in the past, and dupes and knaves will see the light and repent in bitter regret for the false cause they unwittingly served.

Take a long look at the blessings the Divine Creator heaped upon this land. Scarcely 200 years old, we have transformed a prairie land into a paradise where the just may prosper and where each man is to an extent his brother's keeper. A land that has seen the prairie schooner replaced by the aeroplane; the smoke signal by television; and the oxen by the automobile. Man has not done these things by himself. The Bible has retained its place in American life since it sat on the shelf with the pioneer's carbine. God has not been replaced in the hearts and minds of men; Faith has never wavered in the face of adversity and the Godless Ism that is our current threat will fade and disappear as surely as the Kaiser, Hitler, Mussolini and all the other tyrants of history, who for a short time had an evil dream that man can supplant God.

So for myself I thank God for the privilege of living in this land and being a servant of the wonderful people that comprise it. I am grateful that our resources have permitted us to provide for so many of the people of the world. I am confident that the righteousness of this nation will prevail and that our Faith in God will be rewarded and restored to those who do not have it.

"Ciest le Guere"
Remarks by Robert E. Lee
before the
National Association of Broadcasters Convention
Denver, Colorado
October 22, 1976

In this election year, government, including the regulatory agencies, has become a popular focus of criticism. Government is accused of being too big, too much of a sweetheart of the regulated industries, not responsive enough, to consumers, and generally too encumbered with unnecessary regulations. The suggested "cures" for these alleged problems have included dismemberment or consolidation of agencies, automatic expiration of regulations, and, ironically, increased regulatory involvement by existing agencies.

While there are probably isolated horror stories about regulations that don't appear to make much sense on the surface, I think that government has become the scapegoat for many of the dissatisfactions of our everyday lives. Let's face it, society is complicated. The population is growing constantly; technological revolution has become commonplace. Sometimes it seems that just coping with all the confusion of modern society has become our major problem. And, when we become frustrated, we blame the government while asking it to solve our problems.

It's healthy to step back on occasion to question what we are doing and why. It's also healthy to reexamine the role of government. But, it isn't healthy to gripe just for the sake of griping. Nor is it constructive to blame the government or government officials for all of our problems.

The government doesn't exist in a vacuum. It doesn't grow of its own momentum, and it doesn't think of new things to regulate, or new laws and rules in an isolation booth. It has grown and assumed new responsibilities because, in large part, regulated industries and the people have demanded more government involvement.

While I can't comment about agencies I'm not familiar with, I have come to know the FCC after 23 years as a Commissioner. Since government has become such an important issue, I'd like to discuss some of the things the FCC has done with regard to broadcasting -- and why.

The best place to start is with the creation of the FCC. Back in the 1920's, after the discovery of radio broadcasting, a lot of people built and operated AM radio stations. Some beefed up their power, some operated mobile transmitters, some hopped from frequency to frequency, and some did all these things. The 1910 Wireless Ship Act, under which the Secretary of Commerce licensed wireless communication systems, didn't confer adequate authority to handle this increasing chaos. AM radio broadcasting became so interference-ridden that manufacturers, politicians, and others pleaded for a government solution. That solution was creation of the Federal Radio Commission in 1927, and the FCC in 1934, to arbitrate among needs for radio spectrum through allocations to adopt rules governing uses of radio, and to deal with developments as they would come along.

As technology, conflicting demands, and competing interests become more complicated, the FCC's job and, of course, its rules, also become more complicated. On the whole, however, I think the FCC has done an effective job and has carried out its responsibility pursuant to the public interest standard which guides its decisions.

Frequency allocation is one of the Commission's primary responsibilities. After the AM interference problem was cleaned up, the FCC looked into standards for the newly emerging TV technology. It shared with many people a fear that the chaos of AM development might be repeated with television if standards were not adopted quickly. Between 1938, when the Radio Manufacturers Association first urged the adoption of television transmission standards, and 1952 when the Sixth Report and Order allocation table was adopted, the Commission became convinced that television's potential justified a substantial amount of spectrum space in spite of the large number of competing demands for frequency. The Commission also became convinced that twelve VHF channels would not be adequate to fill the need for television service across the country. For this reason, seventy UHF channels were reserved. Unfortunately, these channels were allocated to communities having VHF allocations.

As has been proven by history, the intermixture of U's with V's severely retarded UHF development. It was years before UHF overcame the competitive disadvantages created by its tuning, technical, and psychological problems. In the meantime, the UHF band's propagation characteristics attracted requests for reallocation of channels to nonbroadcast uses. Some erosion took place, but, fortunately, the Commission found an imaginative solution to the problem of nonbroadcast frequencies. Its 900 MHz decision and its present efforts to move away from bloc allocations are, in my opinion, outstanding examples of government responsiveness.

I recognize that decisions like the 900 MHz decision are controversial. Land-mobile users preferred spectrum space in the UHF television band. The UHF band would be easier to use, and, it was argued, cheaper. However, UHF is too valuable to television's continued development to let it slip away. UHF has become the backbone of our educational television system and a Spanish language network. Many stations have upgraded their facilities and now provide picture quality comparable to VHF stations. Many more commercial stations have become profitable in the last few years. But, more important, UHF is the last realistic chance we have for adding more stations to our nationwide television system.

I do agree that we should review our allocations to be sure that they continue to be appropriate in light of technological advances and changing population patterns. For this reason, I support the Commission's plan to establish a UHF task force to develop a comprehensive UHF plan. It is time for the full Commission to recognize UHF's potential, reaffirm its commitment to an expanded television service, and end piecemeal erosion of the band.

In the meantime, I continue to oppose short-sighted proposals, such as VHF drop-ins, which can only undermine the improving outlook of UHF television. UHF's major impediment, the UHF tuning disadvantage, has almost been eliminated. We don't need a new Commission-created psychological disadvantage. If UHF is given a chance to function in a fair competitive environment, I think it will repeat the growth phenomenon we saw with FM radio. I want to give it that chance before killing it off and leaving in its place only a few, low power VHF stations which cause interference to other stations.

Basic allocation decisions such as the one made in the Sixth Report and Order are only one part of the Commission's responsibility. After making the policy judgment inherent in an allocation decision, the Commission must be sure the plan works. To do this, the FCC has adopted technical requirements and equipment standards. This isn't a very glamorous part of the Commission's job, but it is critical. Equipment must operate within the prescribed tolerances to avoid interference. However, equipment design has become much more sophisticated in the last few years. Recognizing that requirements based upon older equipment may be unduly burdensome, the Commission has reviewed and revised or eliminated a substantial number of its rules.

Far more controversial than the Commission's technical standards are the policies adopted to implement the real purpose of broadcast allocation plans, that is, responsive local broadcast services. The bottom line is programming which deals with local needs and interests and current controversial issues. The Commission could, of course, dictate issues or prohibit improper program content as it is frequently asked to do in spite of the First Amendment, but it has chosen a different route to promoting the public interest. That route is guidelines, such as ascertainment to discern community needs, the Fairness Doctrine to insure balanced coverage of controversial issues chosen by the licensee, equal employment opportunity requirements to prevent programming biases which might result from racially unbalanced staffs, program duplication restrictions to increase diversity of radio programming, and even the Prime Time Access Rule to reserve part of the prime time period for licensees.

These policies have been subjects of substantial debate. Some argue the Commission has become too involved in licensee judgment and has too little regard for the broadcaster's willingness to serve the public interest without government prodding. Others point to things like excessive sex and violence in programming to argue that the Commission's standards are not strong enough.

I believe the Commission has reached a good balance between neglect and overregulation. While I support the revisions recently made in ascertainment and the Fairness Doctrine, I do not believe the industry is mature enough today to warrant elimination of such standards. The spectrum is too valuable and the influence of broadcasters too strong for the Commission to ignore its own statutory obligation for insuring use of the spectrum in the public interest.

On the other hand, I don't believe the Commission has any

business acting as a censor, even if the object of censorship is sex and violence rather than political opinion. Such action would be unconstitutional, prohibited by the Communications Act, and poor public policy. This doesn't mean there are no problems with programming or that I condone audience exploitation. However, the problems of censorship are frightening enough that reliance on licensee discretion is the preferable choice. Because the discretion to choose and produce programs does lie with the broadcaster, the broadcaster has an awesome responsibility. The Commission can only challenge broadcasters to exercise their judgment in the best interests of the public. How that judgment is exercised is up to the broadcasters.

Since broadcasters, especially television broadcasters, do have a strong influence on their audiences, my belief in the importance of UHF television is reinforced. More stations will hopefully bring more diversity to programming and more choices for audiences who are tired of the standard program fare. The VHF channels are taken. Without an abundance of UHF channels, the public is not likely to get much more television diversity in today's mass audience competitive environment.

As my remarks here demonstrate, broadcasters, like government, have received their share of criticism. I don't think broadcasters are responsible for all of society's problems, and I don't think broadcasters should be expected to provide instant cures any more than government should. But, it is time for some serious soul searching to be sure judgments are guided by the public interest, not just by ratings. Broadcasters have a lot to contribute. If they contribute all they can, the burdens of government regulation may become unnecessary.

"So Long Pal"
Remarks by Robert E. Lee
Before the National Association of Broadcasters
Las Vegas, Nevada
April 15, 1981

"The time has come," the walrus said,
"To talk of many things:
Of shoes -- and ships -- and sealing wax --
Of cabbages -- and kings --
And why the sea is boiling hot --
And whether pigs have wings."

This bit of whimsy from Lewis Carroll's "The Walrus and the Carpenter" might well be the way for me to lead into what our friends in the media describe as "a few general, wide-ranging comments." As you know doubt know, I am completing 27 years of service at the Federal Communications Commission. I was first appointed in 1953 by President Eisenhower. And I guess you might say I'm on my last legs -- not only as acting chairman but as a commissioner. As the ranking presidential appointee, I hold still another record. The only chairman to enter and to exit as a lame duck. But today I want to speak from my heart about many things, and I hope I am perceived as being humble and yet I must be wary lest I become proud of my humility.

In thinking back over my years at the FCC, I am reminded of what I have come to consider "landmark statements" by several of our chairman when they spoke to this illustrious gathering. You probably recall these pronouncements -- and its possible that you remember them for somewhat different reasons or from entirely different perspectives. In reviewing what these chairman said, I am reminded of the kinds of things we have deemed important as a commission and as an industry.

Larry Fly, in 1940, referred to your illustrious organization as akin to a mackerel in the moonlight. It shines, and it smells.

In 1961, Newton Minnow told us of the "vast wasteland":

> ...when television is bad, nothing is worse. I invite you to sit down in front of your television set when your station goes on the air and stay there without a book, magazine, newspaper, profit and loss sheet, or rating book to distract you -- and keep your eyes glued to that set until the station signs off. I can assure you that you will observe a vast wasteland."

"Topless Radio" was Dean Burch's concern in 1973:

> "...the American commercial broadcast system 'works' just to the extent that public trustees act like public trustees. Sad to say, a few broadcasters today are in the process of rejecting that counsel of caution -- are in fact in the process of forcing a public definition of the fragile distinction between freedom and license. Halfway between here and the bank, however, they may just find themselves in the gutter. The word is apt -- because what I'm talking about, of course, is the latest fad in competitive programming, 'topless' radio and its still relatively uncommon television counterpart, X-rated films."

> "...broadcasters cannot ignore this problem. That in my book is a cop-out, and I cannot square cop-outs with the responsibilities of licensed trustees. You're not buying time, you're buying eventual grief -- and you will all end up paying the price for a handful of your brethren who are deliberately thumbing their noses at good taste and good

sense."

Richard Wiley spoke of a New Ethic in 1974:

> "What I am calling for, ladies and gentlemen, is a
> New Ethic in broadcasting -- a New Ethic which
> fully accepts the opportunity to serve as a public
> trustee and all that it may entail: a New Ethic
> which rejects the concept of engaging in a
> fraudulent practice simply because you probably
> won't get caught; a New Ethic which refuses the
> extra dollar when the cost is to the public; a New
> Ethic which reflects a redirection to principle, a
> redirection to excellence, a redirection to decency,
> a redirection -- indeed -- to the public service."

So now, in 1981, what does your soon to be deposed chairman
offer you -- no gifts this year, only the reminder that your use of
the spectrum is your greatest gift from nature and from God to be
used in the public interest.

These issues and many more like them -- confronting both
broadcasters and the FCC -- have been and will continue to be of
concern to all of us. When we face up to the problem of "a vast
wasteland" and "topless radio" and the necessity of a New Ethic,
we ultimately develop and reinforce standards that must inevitably
lead to performance in the public interest.

I am especially cognizant of how the Commission always
discharges its responsibility mindful of that phrase in the
Communications Act directing it to regulate as "public
convenience, interest or necessity requires." Through many
technological developments and tremendous growth in the
broadcast industry since 1934 the FCC has been guided in its
deliberations and decisions by the public interest standard.

Regulation -- because it usually limits or restricts -- implies a negative relationship between an agency like the FCC and the industry it regulates. Our tendency as individuals -- not as regulator and regulatee -- is to consider all rules bad, when, in fact, we can probably point to many requirements or standards that have helped to improve, protect or more clearly define many aspects of an industry.

Since this may be my swan song, I have no overwhelming desire to decry the industry or even to draw on all precedents and predict in grandiose terms the great things still to come. You in the industry and we at the regulatory agency have seen numerous decisions come and go during my three decades at the FCC. And now with another administration beginning its labors -- many of which you're familiar with by now -- we're beginning yet another phase of that relationship. The atmosphere is now that of a beneficent government emphasizing deregulation, a government striving to lick inflation, achieving those objectives through a government retrenchment program unprecedented certainly in our history. This happens to be a windfall to your industry in the economies inherent in less government oversight. But with it, it seems to me, an obligation for prudent self regulation is on your back. You police not only yourself but you exert pressure on your peers to do likewise.

There is a monastery in Italy where a sign greets a visitor. It says

1.   If a stranger comes to see you, welcome him, he may be a messenger from God.
2.   If he criticizes what you do, listen, it may be God's word.
3.   If he becomes obnoxious or obstreperous, he must be asked to leave.
4.   If he refuses to leave, two strong

monks must explain the will of
God.

In this atmosphere we at the FCC are carefully examining all the
agency's functions. Instead of saying that we can do everything
with fewer resources, we are just not going to do as much.

We may need to take bold steps to do our part in reaching goals
in this new environment. For example, I think we should stop
licensing CB radio and provide for automatic license renewals.
When I testified on the Radio Regulations Act of 1981 I suggested
this and hoped that non-broadcast activities would receive
legislative attention, but I hasten to suggest that the broadcast bill
not be burdened with extraneous matters.

I pointed out that the Commission believes the legislation achieves
significant public interest objectives and paves the way for even
greater public benefits in telecommunications service. The
Commission supports the provisions that establish indefinite
license terms for radio and give the Commission discretion to
grant certain broadcast applications based on a system of random
selection. We did, however, recommend that the bill be enlarged
to permit random selection in all Commission licensing efforts,
including television, common carrier and private radio. A
companion bill has also been introduced to increase TV license
terms to five years and to ensure license renewal absent specific
and serious violations and to eliminate comparative hearings in
new applications.

As to the Commission's recent radio deregulation action, I told the
Senate committee that our basic rationale was the development of
radio broadcasting into a competitive industry where natural
market forces are more effective than Commission regulation in
inducing licensees to act in the public interests and desires, are the
reason radio programming is responsive to the public interest and
why most Americans can receive many radio signals offering a

wide variety of entertainment and informational programs.

Earlier I quoted from statements made to this body by four other commissioners. Without seeming too immodest, I would like to include an observation I made in addressing an NAB convention in Denver in 1976:

> "I don't think broadcasters are responsible for all of society's problems, and I don't think broadcasters should be expected to provide instant cures any more than government should. But it is time for some serious soul-searching to be sure judgments are guided by the public interest, not just by ratings. Broadcasters have a lot to contribute. If they contribute all they can, the <u>burdens of government regulation may become unnecessary.</u>"

A few weeks ago I spoke to the Radio and Television Commission of the Southern Baptist Convention, an organization of religious broadcasters. A few of the points I emphasized on that occasion bear repeating here, for some of the same problems religious broadcasters face are typical of those all broadcasters encounter. I told the gathering that this microphone is, in reality, a gift from God and that we must account for its use or abuse to an authority higher than the FCC. A Supreme being might one day ask you, what you have done with the gift I have given you.

The idea of profit, I said, has somehow become involved with the electronic ministry in recent years. We hear of the accumulation of dollars as often as we hear of the gathering of converts. I also emphasized that the miracle of electronics is not an unmixed blessing, for it includes pornography, violence, exploitation and other programming that appeals to our lowest instincts and debases human experience.

As part of that unmixed blessing I included what might very well be an abuse of the airwaves that is more subtle than sowing the seeds of violence and pornography -- mingling of Biblical teachings with political goals. Of course, we cannot censor or control the content of programs. But that does not mean that those who present secular and religious material bear no responsibility for their programs. I told the religious broadcasters -- and I think I should repeat it here -- that the absence of accountability to government increases the broadcaster's accountability to a higher authority.

We are always accountable to a higher authority when we use this microphone -- this gift from God, as I called it. And our programming decisions should be based on that sense of responsibility. In my record-breaking career I have made many mistakes. Mistakes I bitterly regret. But my advice to you today is not one of them.

This is probably my last opportunity to talk to a significant body of broadcasters. In a manner of speaking, I am bidding farewell to all my friends in the industry. Without getting maudlin, I would like to recall something I have heard said about Hawaii: "To have to leave you is to die a little bit."

May God be with you, but not too soon.

"Requiem for a Regulator"
Remarks by Robert E. Lee
Before the Federal Communications Bar Association
Capital Hilton Hotel
Washington, D.C.
June 10, 1981

There is an appointed time for everything, and a time for every affair under the heavens. A time to be born and a time to die; a time to plant, and a time to uproot the plant. A time to kill, and a time to heal; a time to tear down, and a time to build. A time to weep, and a time to laugh; a time to mourn, and a time to dance. A time to scatter stones, and a time to gather them; a time to embrace, and a time to be far from embraces. A time to seek, and a time to lose; a time to keep, and a time to cast away. A time to rend, and a time to sew; a time to be silent, and a time to speak. A time to love, and a time to hate; a time of war, and a time of peace (Ecclesiastes 3:1-8)

Today is my time to say goodbye to you and the time to speak of what I have learned. I hope you do not find me presumptuous as I attempt to smooth the way for you and my successors.

Telecommunications has been exploding as long as I have been a part of it, and the end is far from in sight. The job of Commissioner, and the job of Chairman, are awesome responsibilities which permeate even one's personal life.

Many years ago, I gave to broadcasters "Ten Commandments" to observe in the operation of a broadcast station. Today, I give Ten Commandments to my colleagues on the Commission, and I hope you who practice before this agency (FCC) will listen because you can make them easier to keep -- or harder. These are not easy to live by. Many of them I have observed in the breach, but for what they are worth, I give them to posterity.

In preparing these commandments I recalled a quotation hanging on a plaque in my mother's kitchen which read as follows:

> There is so much good in the worst of us
> And so much bad in the best of us
> That it behooves none of us
> To speak about the rest of us.

I will now depart from this wise maxim. I hope my commandments speak about the rest of us in a respectful tone and provide help to those who will follow in my footsteps.

1. AVOID CLOSE PERSONAL RELATIONSHIPS WITH LICENSEES, CONGRESSIONAL STAFFS, AND COLLEAGUE COMMISSIONERS.

Many of my friends in this audience know I have violated this principle. If I had to do it over I would act differently. This is not a confession of error since my true friends have never asked me for a favor, nor did they expect to receive one. My experience has been that, over a long period of time, close friendships develop through working relationships. This can cause the undesirable appearance of possible favoritism, a "tilting" to help your friend in a close call.

2. ACCEPT ONLY MODEST ENTERTAINMENT THAT IS BUSINESS RELATED.

I have never had a problem with the occasional lunch or dinner sponsored by members of the regulated industries or their representatives. What is reprehensible to me is that some might think they can bribe through modest entertainment. However, discretion is the order of the day, and even the appearance of impropriety through gifts or lavish or too much entertainment must be avoided. An old maxim could apply: if it's a gift, it is too much; if it's a bribe, it's not enough.

3. KEEP PUBLIC STATEMENTS TO A MINIMUM.

Unless you feel strongly on an issue, you are prudent to avoid total commitment. The issues before the FCC are complex. New information and new perspectives that might very well affect one's judgment have a way of turning up. The best time to make a decision is when one casts the vote.

4. IF YOU DEPART FROM YOUR PRECEDENT, EXPLAIN YOUR REASONING.

The very efficient Communications Bar Association members study individual Commissioner's viewpoints along with the Commission's decisions, and they are sensitive to deviations from the past. Variance should not be avoided, but it most certainly should be explained.

Consistency is not necessarily a virtue. Times and circumstances change, and one must adjust to changing conditions.

Knowing as I do the love of lawyers for consistency, as well as for loopholes, I strongly urge that precedent be an important part, but not necessarily a controlling one, in the decisional process.

5. REJECT REAPPOINTMENT.

Coming from one who has had six presidential appointments in this arena from four different presidents, one might wonder why I say this.

The central theme of the Communications Act is to protect the independence of the agency from both executive and legislative branches.

After my first appointment, Robert T. Bartley, my friend and a former Commissioner, took me to see his uncle, the late venerable Speaker of the House, Sam Rayburn.

Mr. Rayburn, as one of the authors of the Communications Act, told me that, in seeking appointment in the first instance, it is perfectly proper to seek influential Congressional support, but after appointment you should owe absolutely nothing to anyone.

Reappointment should be strictly on merit and the record made by the incumbent. But, of course, it is not, and anyone who believes it is naive in the extreme.

The reappointment process is demeaning. One must go trotting around with hat in hand to the power structure, including the very industry one regulates. I hasten to add I know of no instance where a return of a favor has occurred, but it may have, and, in any event, the appearance is there. I know of no time when the influence of the industry has been greater. I do not necessarily disagree, but I trust this influence will be used discreetly, since excesses have a way of surfacing. We all know the pendulum has a way of swinging back.

To cure the reappointment problem, I have suggested a legislative change whereby the term of office would be changed to 15 years, with a one term limitation. I would couple this with an early retirement provision, and I would remove the limitation on practicing before the Commission. There is precedent for this from the terms for the Comptroller and Deputy Comptroller of the General Accounting Office.

6. BEWARE OF LOG ROLLING.

The restrictive provisions of the so-called Sunshine Act have made informal meeting among a quorum of Commissioners impossible. If Commissioners want to kick around ideas before the time for a final decision, they must do so through a series of one-on-one contacts. Prior to Sunshine we had an informal agreement, sometimes violated, that discussion on particular cases would be conducted only in the presence of all Commissioners. We frequently met in private to have frank discussions about many things. This sort of informality could not be done in public. Now power blocks can develop through "one-on-one" discussions held to line up four votes. This undermines the intended collegiality of the Commission. Also, because Commissioners cannot meet informally, a chairman can have much more control over the agenda. While I'm not saying this is how business is done at the Commission, log rolling can become a problem. How can I vote against a colleague on an issue I am not overly concerned about when he or she has just accommodated me on some other issue?

7. BE CANDID WITH CONGRESS AND THE PRESS. DO NOT COMPOUND AN ERROR.

If there is one area where double talk doesn't work, it is in dealing with Congress and the press. Complete candor is not an unpardonable sin. Neither is admission of error. Your reputation is early established and, if your veracity is in doubt, a bad one will haunt you. As the Supreme Court has said, the fact of concealment is more serious than the fact concealed.

Also avoid the practice of "leaking" to any source about a matter that furthers one's own goals. The press and the Congress may claim to appreciate the "leak", but I am convinced that they understand the motive and do not respect you for it. They will take advantage of you if you become known as a "leak", and they will be the first to criticize you when leaks in particular cases undermine the integrity of the Commission's decision.

8. DO NOT GIVE YOUR WORD LIGHTLY, BUT KEEP IT WHEN YOU GIVE IT.

As a matter of fact, it is a good idea never to commit yourself to a course of action until you are sure all of the information is in and you have been made aware of it. In particular, resist the temptation to tell the crowd only what you think they want to hear in your speeches. You might back yourself into a position you are uncomfortable with at a later date.

9. WATCH YOUR TRAVEL.

Travel is very visible and should not be abused. One should not be flattered by all the speaking engagements that are offered. Perhaps you are asked because you are free entertainment prohibited by ethical concerns from accepting either travel expenses or an honorarium.

As a matter of fact I believe Congress should endorse reimbursement of travel expenses by trade groups and other associations. This could be done through the appropriations process. While travel should not be abused, there are many occasions when Commissioners should speak. Why should the taxpayers be burdened with an expense when private interests are the principal beneficiaries?

10. MAINTAIN AND PROTECT THE INDEPENDENCE OF THE AGENCY.

The Congress created the FCC to be an independent arm of the Congress responsive to their collective will, but not responsible to any member or staff.

Every Commissioner is tested in his or her early days by requests for special attention. Many times these requests are legitimate; they seek redress for unreasonable delay or bureaucratic red tape. Of course one must respond. But, if special favors are granted, the requests never stop and one finds 535 bosses calling the tune.

Some of you may think this advice from the old goat is gratuitous, presumptuous, arrogant -- or all three. And so it may be. The government has been very good to me; you have been good to me. I want all of you who follow in such service to profit from my experiences.

"Go Orbit, Young Man, Go Orbit"
Remarks by Robert E. Lee
Upon Receiving an Honorary Doctorate Degree
at the Graduation Commencement
St. Bonaventure University
Olean, New York
May 15, 1983

Mr. President, Reverend Clergy, Graduates and Friends. Commencement addresses are supposed to be impassioned exhortations to inspire the embarking graduate students with a shining face and still warm sheepskin to go out and conquer the world. My brief remarks are indeed no exception.

Horace Greeley lived in the last century, a prominent journalist, Congressman and Presidential candidate, who implored young people with his now famous rallying cry, "Go West, Young Man, Go West!" This was a time when new frontiers were opening and opportunity beckoned to those who had the will and the fortitude to brave all of the adversities of weather, hostilities, disease and famine. There were and are none who deplored that advice. The young and brave who survived, prospered, and empires were built and a wilderness opened for the poorest people of the Earth who fled from tyranny and helped to develop this vast land that we call our own.

If Horace Greeley were here today, he would not say: "Go West;" he would not say "Go East;" he would not say "Go North;" nor would he say "Go South." He would say today, "Go Up, Young Person, Go Up!" Space is the new frontier. It is where you will find your future and make your contribution to the generations as yet unborn.

You were an infant or perhaps unborn when Russia put into space a satellite called "Sputnik" that roused this country into unprecedented entry in the space age leading to a secure leadership in this latest gift from God.

Your generation has seen this miracle, which is only part of the continuing process in the technological progress that has had more development in my lifetime than in all of recorded history before me.

Yes, you have seen not the conquest of space, but only the opening of a new vista. The end of which can be predicted only in the imagination.

To my certain knowledge, I will probably see cities in the sky and you will certainly see them. Who will be there and what will they be doing? Only you can answer that.

A lifetime is only a minuscule particle in time and before you know it you will be here speaking to a new generation of graduates who are not as yet a glimmer in their parents' eyes. What will you tell them? Will you tell them of an obscure individual who ushered or perhaps inspired you to go into the space age?

We all remember our first adventures into space. How we were glued to our television sets to experience the spine-tingling emotion of pride in the United States. We honored the first astronauts, electing them to high office and giving them other special privileges bestowed on national heroes. We now know that one of them aspires to be President (John Glenn). But I cannot help but reflect how quickly we came to accept these wondrous feats. Our latest adventure in space, the shuttle ship, Challenger, was by far the most successful, and it re-entered earth on April 9, 1983. [Collaborator's Note: this speech was before the Challenger disaster.]

As I watched the four astronauts emerge, I mused how casually we all accept them. I wondered how many would be on the next flight. Is it straining credulity to say that next year there will be dozens of astronauts, and in the next decade, hundreds of space travelers, and then thousands traveling to and from a city in space where they work on a variety of projects that are not presently conceivable based on our current knowledge. I venture to say that there are those among you who will be among them.

My point is simple. Make the most of your time on earth and finish your brief term in the realization that the God-given talents that were gifts to you have been enhanced a thousand times. It is your turn to put your imprint on generations yet to come, and so it goes "ad infinitum."

Take pride in what you do, but with humility.

"The Marketplace Must Be Policed"
Discussion Notes of
Robert E. Lee
Before the
California Broadcasters Association
Monterey, California
July 27, 1987

Having participated in a multitude of de-regulatory decisions under several FCC Chairman -- from Dean Burch on down -- I feel more than a little sheepish at having to confess that, in retrospect, perhaps the FCC has gone a little too far and that it is time for the FCC to tighten-up before Congress reacts to a growing number of serious complaints, and takes the law into its own hands.

Without criticizing anybody, and admitting honestly that I may have even been part of the problem, I now believe that unless the FCC begins to reassess some of its de-regulatory initiatives taken over the past decade-and-a-half, the calls for Congressional action against the FCC will be overpowering -- and successful in ways that will put the broadcast industry under tighter constraints than ever before in its history.

I agree with the past FCC Chairman -- including Mark Fowler and, now, Dennis Patrick -- that marketplace competition is a very useful tool to help ensure public protection. Our American economic system depends greatly on the "invisible hand" of competition to regulate many business practices -- and both products and services. But, it cannot altogether replace legal and regulatory provisions that are necessary to guarantee that the marketplace is not manipulated, overrun, exploited, and ultimately ruined by those who would put their thumbs on the scale, or cut corners, or -- in fact -- commit any fraud or other misconduct they think they can get away with. Unfortunately, the crooks of this world -- like the poor -- will always be with us.

And we ought to here take a lesson from history, <u>ancient and recent</u>, and recall that the world's <u>first real marketplace</u> -- the Market Square which served from biblical times down through the middle ages -- finally had to be abandoned in larger, modern societies because the merchants increasingly became nothing more than roving brigands; the goods became shoddy and spoiled; and there was no recourse after the dishonest merchants packed-up and scurried to distant towns (or even across the border). In fact, it got so bad that the crooks would hire jugglers, or jesters, or even signers to mesmerize the crowds, while their henchmen roamed the square picking pockets and shoplifting from the few honest merchants still left. Because innocent consumers could no longer trust the ancient Market Square, merchants eager to demonstrate honesty and reliability moved out of the Market Square and migrated progressively into more permanent storefronts.

<u>What I am saying is this</u>: No "marketplace" -- whether it was the Old Market Square, or the New York Stock Market, or the <u>communications marketplace</u> -- can continue to function if respectable businessmen and ordinary customers are not protected from thieves, con-men, and fast-buck artists. <u>Nobody</u> will come into a corrupt "marketplace" to transact business and -- just like the bygone medieval Market Square -- a <u>disreputable</u> marketplace will surely die. And to prove my point, ask yourselves seriously just how long your closest shopping mall would survive if it became overrun by sleazy merchants, pickpockets, prostitutes, pimps, dope dealers, muggers, or other assorted fly-by-night operators. Not very long, I assure you; and you know it too!

And, I'm afraid we're beginning to see that very phenomenon in the broadcast industry: licensees who buy today and sell tomorrow; raunch radio; dishonest clergymen; sham license applicants; program-length toy commercials intended to greedily exploit six-year-olds; and fraudulent coverage maps. All of you <u>know</u> it, and many of you are suffering losses because of it. All it eventually does is to force you <u>to sink to the level of your most unscrupulous competitor</u> -- <u>or loose out.</u> <u>Some choice</u>!

I may be old-fashioned, but I do not want to see the broadcasting business permanently trashed; I do not want to let the <u>bad</u> drive out the <u>good</u>! I don't want the lowest common-denominator to prevail! And to ensure that good broadcasters are not compelled by business necessity to abandon the decent standards of their own consciences, the FCC must again help police the broadcast marketplace -- or that marketplace must ultimately die of its own internal rot! Just the same as any other.

You know, for the almost 28 years I served on the FCC, I found that 95 percent of all broadcasters I met were good and faithful trustees of the public interest. And that most broadcasters I encountered <u>proudly</u> considered themselves to hold a very "<u>special</u>" place in our American society. Not only the great leaders of the industry: people like Bob Sarnoff, Bill Paley, Len Goldenson, Stan Hubbard, J. Leonard Rensch, Tom Murphy, and Don McGannon. But almost <u>all</u> of the broadcasters I met in nearly three decades on the FCC were honest and dedicated professionals trying "to do <u>well</u> by doing <u>good</u>!" And I believe that most of the broadcasters here today do not see themselves -- <u>or want to see themselves</u> -- as down-and-dirty "fast-buck" artists or Coney Island communicators. I still see broadcasters as very "<u>special</u>" individuals who hold a tremendously valuable <u>privilege</u> granted by the people of the United States. And who have a duty to use that license -- at least part of the time -- to serve the public interests of their cities, their towns, and their local communities. I <u>always</u> thought broadcasters were a very "special" class of people -- <u>and I still think they are,</u> and should be treated as such. And held to a higher ethical standard than the corner used-car dealer.

But if you wish to be <u>treated</u> "specially," then you must <u>act</u>

"specially" -- or else forfeit your right to things like "must carry," or "syndicated exclusively," or keeping your frequencies away from land mobile users.

As for the FCC, In sincerely think its time to take a second look at <u>some</u> of the results of accumulated deregulation, and to reconsider whether certain of these changes made things better -- or actually worse. Shouldn't we have really adopted a single nationwide AM Stereo standard -- or has our abdication unwittingly killed off AM radio? Shouldn't we require television set manufacturers -- under the "All-Channel Receiver Rules" -- to have an "A/B" switch so that the public can easily shift to their local off-the-air channels if they wished? And shouldn't we quickly put back in place the "Three-Year Rule" to ward off the hit-and-run types that could easily transform the broadcasting profession into nothing much better than a back-alley crap game?

As I've said, maybe I share the blame for some of the bad things that have started to happen to this industry in the wake of deregulation. And even though certain station prices have risen substantially in some areas, I also see many broadcasters losing out badly. For example, network ownership is down to only 73 percent of the prime-time audience; scores of UHF independents are going bust because they can't afford competitive or exclusive product; AM stations are being auctioned off for peanuts; broadcast frequencies are being handed away to non-broadcast spectrum users; pioneer broadcasters like Taft -- and Storer before it -- are folding forever or else being gobbled-up by greedy stock manipulators.

And I say to all of my dear friends in this industry <u>and</u> on the FCC, let's take another look -- and see if we can help get back to the truly great days of this dynamic, vital industry when broadcasters <u>and</u> the government "did <u>well [together]</u> by doing <u>good</u>."

APPENDIX 2

THE USE OF HUMOR

[Collaborator's Note: Like President Ronald Reagan, Bob Lee
was a student of humor, possessing an encyclopedic memory of
thousands of jokes and humorous stories. He even kept an
extensive joke file. he believed that jokes could often drive home
a point more effectively than abstract statistics or dry scientific
data. Humor spoke of the human condition, and connected with
people. But as many of his friends and colleagues have noted,
Mr. Lee never told a joke at someone's expense. He never
employed humor to be painful or biting. Instead, through the use
of carefully selected stories and jokes, in Mr. Lee's hands humor
was a "safe" subject that traversed the common ground possessed
by a particular audience, building bridges of understanding and
warmth, and inspiring the listening audience to engage in acts of
sacrifice and service. Again and again, those who knew Mr. Lee
stress his masterful ability to tell a story, his twinkling eyes, his
engaging smile, and his impeccable timing. Some attribute his
abilities to his Irish heritage (Judge Lee Lovenger, former FCC
Commissioner, claims that Mr. Lee's humor was principally a
product of the well-known Irish tradition of "kissing the blarney
stone"). Others see Mr. Lee's abilities as a practiced, thorough
study of the human condition. What is clear is that Mr. Lee was
a humorist, and jokes were weapons in the battle for the mind. In
his speeches, there are personal notations to employ certain stories

or jokes (i.e. "Time permitting go to Uncle Mike" or "Dr. Spock and the cornflake story"). In his briefing notes for meetings, often each point in an argument that he wanted to make was followed by notations for a story or joke (such as "robin story" or "105-year-old Irish lady"). Humor was used to bond with an audience, to illuminate serious truths, to relieve tensions in meetings, to make nervous petitioners relax, to paint a mental picture, and to fill in the time.

Mr. Lee was often compared to one of his favorite comedians, Danny Thomas. When they once both appeared on the same program, Mr. Lee pulled out all the stops, leaving the room shaking with laughter and his role model in tears.

In the following passage, placed here in an appendix for the reader, is a manuscript on humor left by Mr. Lee. These thoughts were used in several speeches after he retired from the FCC, and formed the springboard for a series of jokes that followed. These jokes built to a climax of great one-liners at the end. It shows his thoughtful approach to this great, timeless subject.]

***

The word "humor" is basically a Latin word meaning fluids of the body. In ancient physiology the four cardinal fluids of the body were blood, phlegm, choler, and melonchology. The proper mix of these elements, or the state of being in good humor, was a matter of physical well-being. A disproportionate mixture of these fluids produced a different person, or persons, when the mixtures were changed. For example, a man could be sanguine, phlegmatic, choleric, or melancholic, depending on the ratios of the mixtures.

In modern times we have forgotten this view of humor, but it was well known in earlier times. Shakespeare often employed this view in his plays, and humor in the Renaissance period actually denoted an unbalanced mental condition.

For some, humor was a vice, as was well illustrated in the best-selling book, <u>The Name of the Rose</u>.

Ben Johnson found that humor was something of an affectation. At the end of the seventeenth century, the term began to be a compliment, referring to a person of extremes.

On the other hand, wit began to emerge at this time as the quality of a rake -- one who scoffed at religion, marriage, or tradition. Wit required learning.   It was equated with cleverness and irreverence.

Humor was a more natural gift. For many centuries, humor was relegated to the lower classes. It became amusing and innocent. It was associated with singing, good nature, and love. It was even felt to be a guise to hide tender feelings.

But, eventually humor became established as the highest form of comedy. For example, in our time a humorist is someone who is skilled in comic artistry. The term is also applied to the ability of the audience to perceive or appreciate comedy.

In my own life I began to wonder what made people laugh. After all, what's so funny about a man falling on ice or a woman who is hit by a falling pail or water? So, in search of an answer, I began a study of humor. For instance, I found that Cambridge University researched this problem and developed a series of stories to test for a sense of humor. They found that it was important to know an audience beforehand, to actually understand what made an audience laugh or what made that same audience apprehensive. The researchers suggest that one carefully examine and classify an audience, mixing a potent of stories to match the mood of an audience.

That is all very academic, but there surely is a great need for audience adaptation. In my own experience, I have found that an audience has a certain personality, and manifests its won dynamic qualities. The speaker can feel the audience's energy and excite (or lack of it) while listening to the introduction, or while walking to the podium. The first few seconds of a speech reveal volumes as you set the stage for your presentation.

So I would test an audience with my first joke or story, trying to see where they were and what they wanted to hear. Then I would adjust my presentation accordingly, fine-tuning my style to fit the pathos developing between speaker and audience.

As the veteran of hundreds of conventions, and listening to thousands upon thousands of speeches, and well as giving several thousand of my own, I earnestly tried to collect as many jokes and stories as I could. Often I would study my joke file for hours, picking the right joke for the point I wished to make, and then working on my delivery to make the joke seem oft-hand and spontaneous. Many on my staff would say I worked harder on the jokes than on the serious part of my speech. But I didn't distinguish between the two. Jokes have more than an appeal -- they have a persuasive power -- the power to change behavior and the power to build consensus. In my long, record-breaking years at the FCC, I learned that jokes could be employed in many ways to get results. And they were a lot of fun -- both for me and for those who were afraid of a dry speech that represented a civilized form of verbal torture. I hope that I made my views known with grace and good cheer.

Here are a few of the jokes I enjoyed telling, and I hope audiences enjoyed hearing:

"As the cow said to the farmer on a cold and frosty morning, thank you for that warm hand."

"Recently, I was introduced after a long cocktail hour, and the speaker gave the same introduction twice. The trouble is, nobody noticed."

"One guy may have noticed -- he was a strange Irishman. He liked women more than whiskey."

"I'm Robert E. Lee -- and I'm not the general."

"Robert Emmet was the father of an Irish patriot. He was tried for collaboration against the British. His stunning courtroom speech has been widely quoted by Irishmen around the world. In a sense, Robert Emmet is the name of all Irishmen."

"But the first Robert Emmet was hanged and beheaded. I guess they wanted to be sure."

"I've kept my head -- so far."

"While both from Ireland, my mother and father were married here. They were surprised to learn that they were married by a rabbi -- a reformed rabbi. In fact, he was so reformed that he was a Jesuit."

"My father used to ask: What if all the politicians were killed and laid end to end, what would you have. Answer: A good idea."

"Dad often said: In my house I'm the boss! My wife has authorized me to say so."

"I went to an Irish store and asked for a newspaper. The proprietor asked 'Do you want yesterday's or today's?' 'Today's,' I replied. 'Then come back tomorrow!'"

"An Irishman came home drunk. His wife asked, 'Why did you come home?' He replied 'It was the only place open.'"

"That same Irishman quit AA and joined AAA. Now he gets towed from bars."

"An Irishman came into a bar and shouted 'Who painted my donkey green?' A big ox of a man stood up and shouted 'Me!' The Irishman took a good long look at him and said 'The first coat is dry.'"

"I heard about an Irishman who drank a quart of whiskey and went to church Jewish."

"In Ireland familiarity breeds contempt...and also children."

"Retirement is a funny thing. Without the government per diem, you start reading the menu from left to right."

"It's strange how retirement from government can affect your golf game. For 44 years I never lost a golf match. Everyone was very solicitous when your ball was lost, and everyone gathered around to help find a lost ball. Since the day of my retirement I have never won a golf match and when I lose my ball I shout 'has anyone seen my ball," and the answer I generally get back is, 'Find your own ball you ex-bureaucrat!'"

"When you retire, you pick up a buck here and a buck there -- which is another way of saying you are out of work."

"What does a lobbyist have to sell? Well, they wine and dine Congressman and Federal regulators, who vote like they would have anyway."

"I must say that I do have some influence in Washington. I don't have to sit in the lobby waiting for an appointment. They make me stand."

"This audience is so good, I wish I was out there listening."

"May God be with you. But not too soon."

####

APPENDIX 3

THE HONORS OF A LIFETIME

Honorary Titles

1. Honorary Membership, Order of the Alaskan Sourdough
2. Honorary Membership, Institute of Electrical and Electronic Engineers
3. Admiral of the Flagship Fleet, American Airlines
4. Colonel in the Confederate Air Force
5. Wyoming Bronc Buster
6. Sagamore of the Wabash, State of Indiana
7. Honorary Citizen of the City of New Orleans
8. Honorary Citizenship of Texas
9. Honorary Citizenship of Louisville, Kentucky

Professional Awards

1. Citation of Excellence, Department of Communication, Fordham University
2. Citation of Excellence, Department of Radio and Television, Indiana University
3. Marconi Gold Medal, Quarter Century Wireless Association
4. Sol Taishoff Award, Washington Area Broadcasters Association

5. Spirit of Broadcasting Award, National Association of Broadcasters
6. Distinguished Service Award, Radio Club of America, Inc.
7. Outstanding Service Award, Radio and Telecommunications Council of Greater Cleveland
8. Distinguished Public Service Award, Association of Federal Communication Consulting Engineers
9. Recognition Award, Broadcast Pioneers Association
10. Distinguished Service Award, Maryland-District of Columbia-Delaware Broadcasters Association

Religious Honors

1. Award of Merit, Catholic Apostolate of Mass Media
2. Distinguished Communicators Award, "Communicating the Breath of Life" Award, Southern Baptist Radio and Television Convention
3. Distinguished Service Award, Brent Society (award shared with Mrs. Lee)
4. Invested as a Knight of Malta, Sovereign Military Order of Malta, Federal Association, United States of America

Honorary Degrees

1. Doctor of Law, St. John's University, New York, New York
2. Doctor of Law, Notre Dame University, South Bend, Indiana
3. Doctor of Science, St. Bonaventure, Olean, New York

DATE DUE
